Furniture and Draperies After the Era of Jane Austen

Ackermann's Repository

OF

ARTS, LITERATURE, COMMERCE,

Manufactures, Fashions, and Politics

1821 - 1828

Designed and Edited by
Jody Gayle

📖 *Publications of the Past*

Publications of the Past, Inc.
Post Office Box 233
Columbia, MO 65205

For further information email
jody@jodygayle.com
or visit
www.JodyGayle.com

ISBN-13: 978-09884001-0-8
Cover: A Cloak-Stand and Flower-Stand from *Ackermann's Repository of Arts*, July 1822

Acknowledgements

My sincerest gratitude to the Philadelphia Museum of Art Library for permission to reintroduce the two-hundred-year-old *Ackermann's Repository of Arts* to a whole new group of readers.

A special thank you to the authors of Regency era fiction, who have continued to make the society, customs and fashions of early nineteenth century England vivid and vital to several generations of readers.

Contents

The rooms were lofty and handsome, and their furniture suitable to the fortune of their proprietor; but Elizabeth saw, with admiration of his taste, that it was neither gaudy nor uselessly fine; with less of splendour, and more real elegance, than the furniture of Rosings.

-- Jane Austen, *Pride and Prejudice*

To learn about fashionable English furniture used in the early nineteenth century, one must dedicate some time to the highly popular publication *Ackermann's Repository of Arts*. The complete title, *Repository of Arts, Literature, Commerce, Manufactures, Fashions and Politics* was a monthly British periodical published from 1809-1828 by Rudolph Ackermann. This widely read publication contained articles devoted to the study of the arts, literature, commerce, manufacturing, politics and fashion. Each issue had of 60-80 pages, and included a significant amount of information provided by the readers, such as personal narratives, poems, opinion pieces and general interest articles.

The *Repository of Arts* frequently featured a section titled "Fashionable Furniture" that created an archive of superb hand-colored aquatint plates that depicted the latest fashions in furniture and draperies and included a description or general narrative on home design. In the 1809, *Ackermann's Repository* pointed out that "the sofa is an indispensible piece of furniture it not only ornaments, but becomes a comfort when tired and fatigued with study, writing, and reading – the exhausted mind can only be recruited by the occasional rest."

These illustrations were used as a guide to craftsmen and their clients in which the client could use the illustrations to order furniture, while selecting a particular fabric, color style and accessories. From 1809 to 1820, there were 144 issues of the *Repository of the Arts* published, and of those, just fewer than one hundred issues included furniture and drapery plates—every illustration is included in this book. Even after two hundred years after the era of Jane Austen we are still delighted and inspired by nineteenth century England. The illustrations in the *Repository of Arts* magazine were mainly for the haute ton, the very wealthy or newly-wealthy; however, they still drove what was considered fashionable at other levels of society. Jane Austen was certainly aware of the *Repository of Arts* magazine and perhaps used its pages to help develop her timeless stories.

The intent of this pictorial is to offer images exclusively from *Ackermann's Repository of Arts*. This book provides readers the opportunity to study the furniture and drapery plates from the era of Jane Austen, as well as read the original accompanying descriptions and narratives. It is important to note the descriptions are as they appeared in the magazine. The punctuation, spelling, sentence structure and even word usage sometimes varied from one issue to the next.

Considerable effort has been directed at precisely providing the text as it was originally written. The text is kept as it was published and the etchings have also not been altered.

Ackermann's Repository of Arts

The following article was first published in the first issue of the
Repository of Arts: January 1809.

This plate is a representation of Mr. Ackermann's Shop, No. 101, Strand, and is the commencement of a series of plates intended to exhibit the principal shops of this great metropolis, in the same manner as the *Microcosm of London* represents the interior of the *public* buildings. It will afford the opportunity of entering into a partial detail of the different manufactures that are exposed in them for sale; and we flatter ourselves will form an useful, as well as interesting, part of our work. This shop stands upon part of the court-yard in front of which was Beaufort-House, formerly a town residence of the noble family whose name it bore, and was one of the great number of mansions which, at no very distant period, lined the bank of the Thames from Templebar to the city of Westminster. The noble and lofty apartments of the house, which commences at the back part of the shop, and a fine oak staircase of considerable dimensions, hear a testimony of its former magnificence. After it had ceased to be the residence of the Beaufort family, it was converted into the Fountain Tavern, a house of great celebrity in former days, and was remarkable from the circumstance of Lord Lovat stopping there to take in refreshment on his way from Westminster-Hall to the Tower, and writing with his diamond ring the following couplet upon a pane of glass in the great room:

> Oh! through what various scenes of life we run,
> Are wicked to great and being great undone!
> Simon Fraser

This room, which is 65 feet in length, 30 in width, and 24 in height, was formerly occupied by Mr. Shipley, brother to the bishop of that name; he kept a most respectable drawing academy here: among his pupils were, Mr. W Parr, who died at Rome, C. Smart, Esq. and the celebrated R. Cosway, Esq. R.A.: the latter had in his possession the pane of glass before-mentioned. A curious, but well-authenticated anecdote is related of Henry Parr's wife (H. Parr succeeded Shipley in this academy) who had been confined to the house upwards of nine years by a paralytic affection, which during that period entirely deprived her of speech. One day, in the absence of her husband, the servant-maid abruptly entering her apartment, told her that the adjoining house was on fire, which had such an effect upon her system, that her powers of utterance returned instantaneously, and she continued to enjoy them again to the day of her death, which did not happen for some year afterwards.

This room is famous on another account, having been the scene of Mr. Thelwall's early political lectures. When the interposition of government put a stop to this exhibition, Mr. A. purchased the lease, and it became once more the peaceful academy of drawing, upon a very extended scale, employing three masters in the separate branches of this art, one for figures, a second for landscape, and a third for architecture. But the increase of Mr. Ackermann's business as a publisher, printseller, and manufacturer of fancy articles, rendered the convenience of this room a warehouse a more desirable object than the profit to be derived from it as an academy. For eight or ten years previous to entering so largely in the fancy business, Mr. A. had been employed in furnishing the principal coachmakers with designs and models for new and improved carriages. Among many instances of his taste and abilities in this line, the state coach built for the Lord Lieutenant of Ireland, in 1790, which cost near 7000/. and one for the Lord Mayor of Dublin in the following year, were designed and modelled by him. It has been said, that Philip Godsal, Esq. who has the model of the Lord Lieutenant's coach, has actually refused one hundred guineas for it, and it is more than probable, he would not sell it for twice that sum.

During the period when the French emigrants were so numerous in this country, Mr. A. was among the first to strike out a liberal and easy mode of employing them, and he had seldom less than fifty noble, priests, and ladies of distinction, at work upon screens, card-racks, flower-stands, and other ornamental fancy-works of a similar nature. Since the decree permitting the return of the emigrants to France, this manufacture has been continued by native artists, who execute the work in a very superior style: but it is impossible in this place to notice the great variety of articles which it embraces. The public are referred to a catalogue of near 100 pages, which conveys every information that can be necessary, and will be our apology for omitting any further observations; we shall therefore only add, that since Mr. A. has given up the academy, he has substituted a portfolio of prints and drawings for the use of pupils and dilitanti, upon the plan of a circulating library of books, the terms of which areas follow: Yearly subscription.

4 Guineas,

Half-yearly ditto.. 2 ditto.

Quarterly ditto... I ditto.

The money paid at the time of subscribing. The subscribers are allowed to take the value of their subscription money in prints or drawings, and may change them as often as they please.

A Dress Sofa
February 1821

A DRESS SOFA

This elegant essential to the drawing-room is after the design of Mr. J. Taylor, who has obtained considerable experience in furniture in the house of Oakley of Bond-street. For decorations of the higher class, the frame-work would be entirely gilt in burnished and matt gold; the pillows and covering of satin damask or velvet, relieved by wove gold lace and tassels. For furniture of less splendour, the frame would be of rose-wood, with the carved work partially gilt, and the covering of more simple materials.

The loom of our country is now in that state of advanced perfection, that damasks of the most magnificent kind, in point of intensity of colour and richness of pattern, are manufactured at prices that permit their free use in well-furnished apartments; and so completely do they compare with the quality of the best foreign articles in all other respects, that there is no doubt but our own will supersede the foreign market, so soon as this fact is generally known. This advancement has been some years in progress, and its first and chief encouragement has been received from Carlton Palace, where for a long time all the damasks employed for its best furniture have been the produce of British art.

GOTHIC SIDEBOARD
July 1821

GOTHIC SIDEBOARD

The design of this elegant and useful piece of furniture was made by Mr. J. Taylor, who has had considerable experience in decorations of the higher class in the house of Oakley of Bond-street.

The sideboard should be made entirely of mahogony, or of fine oak, which has been so generally adopted of late in mansions furnished in the ancient style. This in fact is the more consistent, and therefore the more tasteful, mode of decoration; for in matters of this kind, consistency is absolutely essential to tasteful decoration. Mahogany, however, may he used with great propriety, and perhaps the effect of that wood on the whole is richer than that produced by oak. Of course, however, the adoption of the one or the other must depend upon a variety of circumstances.

The cellaret, which has been made in the form of a sarcophagus, is an imitation of one represented on a tomb in Luton church; and of course it should be made to correspond in size and appearance with the other parts of the sideboard. The shields are well adapted to receive carvings of family arms, which would add greatly to the richness and appearance of the whole.

5

Library Side and Pier Tables
October 1821

LIBRARY SIDE AND PIER TABLES

The simplicity of style manifest in the annexed designs makes them suitable furniture for a book-room or library: the pier-table design is readily convertible to a central one, and by increasing its diameter, the book-pedestal beneath would be usefully enlarged. A similar table in marble or bronze would be proper for a dairy or conservatory; indeed, its form and unostentatious pretensions fit it for many apartments in which simplicity and elegance are united.

The side table forms a case of drawers to contain maps, plans, and other papers not suited to the portfolio, and having a sliding shelf near the top, it becomes a convenient means for their inspection: for preserving prints, however, portfolios are preferable, because the paper suited to receive copper-plate impressions is necessarily soft, and exceedingly liable to injury by removal. The above designs may be executed in any of the superior woods, embellished with or-moulu.

A Chimney-Piece
November 1821

A CHIMNEY-PIECE

 The annexed design of a Mona marble chimney-piece is proposed to be embellished with brass ornaments, and mouldings gilt, or lackered in the present greatly improved process. The receptacle for a register stove is here added, and so as to appear part of the decoration as designed in the first instance, rather than, as is commonly the case, seem to be one chimney-piece within another. The persons who manufacture stoves or grates having nothing to do with the marble work, seek to make their articles sightly, without reference to the superior decoration with which they are destined to unite; and if the parties who select grates for apartments are equally regardless of the forms to which they are proposed to be appended, there need be no wonder at the absurd *mélanges* that become the unavoidable consequences of such inattention to fitness and propriety.

 It rarely happens in common apartments that this defect does not appear, for it is always much more easy to satisfy the fancy than to consult the understanding.

A Girandole for a Mantel-Piece or Pier Table
December 1821

A GIRANDOLE FOR A MANTEL-PIECE OR PIER TABLE

The girandole represented in the accompanying plate is a peculiarly elegant piece of furniture, and is the manufacture of Messrs. Pellatt and Green, of St. Paul's Church-yard.

It is principally formed of glass richly cut, but we would particularly direct the attention of our readers to the ornaments by which it is decorated. The figures and medallions are what are termed glass incrustations over a white composition, which shines through them with the appearance of boiled silver, and producing a splendid and elegant effect. It is designed for two lights, and the vase, in the centre, is placed there to hold flowers, whether artificial or natural.

Messrs. Pellatt and Green have very recently obtained a patent for what they term the *crytallo ceramie*, or glass incrustation, which is made to cover the species of composition used in the ornaments of the annexed design, which may or may not be coloured to imitate mosaic or enamel, with the utmost exactness and the greatest brilliancy. Upon this interesting subject, Mr. Apsley Pellatt, jun. has published an interesting " Memoir," in which he also touches, with much research and accuracy, upon the origin, progress, and improvement of glass-manufactures, in most of the countries of the globe. In consequence of the pressure of temporary matter, we are under the necessity of postponing until our next Number, a quotation we had intended to have made from this curious publication, and which would give a more distinct and satisfactory account of the nature of the beautiful invention which
Messrs. Pellatt and Green have brought to such perfection.

For the present, we must content ourselves with observing, that both the composition (which may be applied in various important ways, as we shall hereafter more fully explain), and the incrustation above it, by which the valuable designs are absolutely perpetuated, are entirely new in this country. In
France they are partially known, but have not been brought there to any considerable degree of excellence.

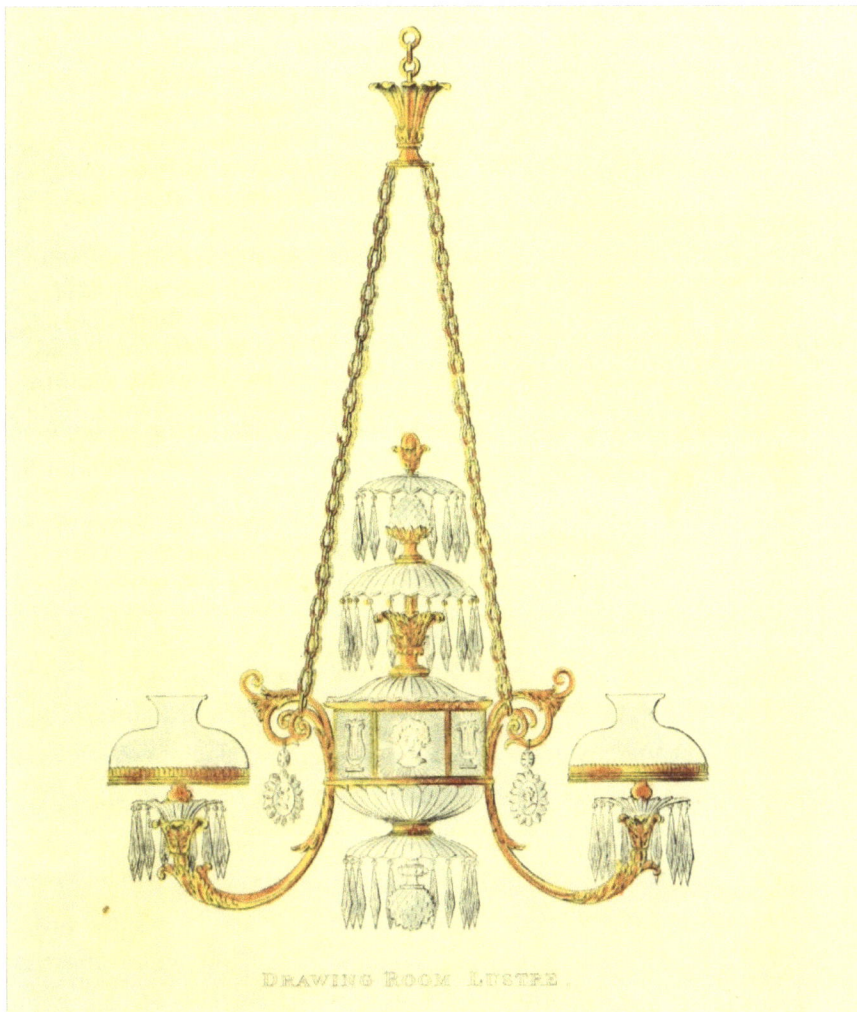

A Drawing-Room Lustre
January 1822

A DRAWING-ROOM LUSTRE

    Although the lustre represented in the annexed plate is not so splendid a piece of furniture as the girandole given last month, its shape is at least quite as elegant, and it is adapted to more general use. It is, like the girandole, the manufacture of Messrs. Pellatt and Green of St. Paul's Church-yard, and the ornaments peculiar to it are of their patent *crystallo ceramie*, or glass incrustation. These ornaments, it will be observed, consist of a head of Apollo between lyres, and in two suspended pieces of glass are additional subjects, all formed of the metallic composition, incrusted over with the glass, and producing a most rich and striking appearance

    It is to be observed, that the larger the scale upon which the lustre is made, the better will be the effect of the *crystallo ceramie*, and if it be displayed by means of French lamps, as in the accompanying plate, the incrustations will be set off to the utmost advantage by means of the intense and powerful light thrown upon them.

    In our last we were too much circumscribed for room to be able to introduce any specimen of the small work to which we referred, by Mr. Apsley Pellatt, junior, entitled "A Memoir of the Origin, Progress, and Improvement of Glass Manufactures," which includes an account of the patent *crystallo ceramie*, of which we have spoken. As we have now a small space illustration of this interesting subject, we gladly avail ourselves of it to quote some passages from the tract above-mentioned, which give particulars regarding the introduction and advantages of this new invention. The author, after cursorily going through the history of glass-manufactures generally, proceeds as follows:

"Glass was first used by the Italians for the purpose of making cameos and intaglios, by impressing it while warm into a mould of tripoli: the glass is sometimes filled up behind with plaster of Paris. Foreigners visiting Italy are thus supplied with copies of antique gems for the formation of cabinet collections. They seldom exceed, however, an inch in diameter, and perhaps could not be made much larger. The manufacture of these artificial gems has been very successfully carried on by Mr. Tassie of Leicester-square, whose collection is extensive and valuable.

"The first English glass-houses for the manufacture of fine flint glass were those of the Savoy and Crutched Friars, established about the middle of the 16th century. It appears, however, that the English manufactures were for a considerable time much inferior to the Venetian; for in 1635, nearly a hundred years later, Sir Robert Mansel obtained a monopoly for importing the fine Venetian flint drinking-glasses. The art of making these was not brought to perfection in this country till the reign of William III. Since then, the art of glass-making has made a rapid progress, and the glass-works of England indisputably excel at this moment those of any other country in the world. The essential and distinguishing qualities of good glass are, its freedom from specks or rings, and its near resemblance to real crystal in its *colourless transparency*. In both these respects, the productions of the British glass-houses exceed those of any other nation. It only remained for them to evince their superiority in the ornamental branches of the art; and this has been fully accomplished by the perfection to which recent discoveries have enabled them to carry the art of incrustation.

"The ancients, we have seen, were not altogether ignorant of this art, but their incrustations were very imperfect. The picture of a duck, described by Winkelman, is but a partial incrustation, as the painting is neither completely inclosed nor protected from the air. The Venetian ball and the Bohemian ornamental stems are perfect incrustations, but they are curious rather than useful. It was impossible to introduce into them any device or figure, which was the desideratum in the art, because the variegated glass in the interior, being of the nature of enamel, is (especially the opaque) fusible at a less degree of heat than the coating of white transparent glass: consequently, any impression must have been effaced, when, in the process of manufacture, it became incased in the hot transparent glass. To render the art of incrustation subservient to any useful purpose, it was requisite, in the first instance, to discover a substance capable of uniting with glass, but requiring a stronger heat to render it fusible.
"About forty years ago, a Bohemian manufacturer first attempted to incrust in glass small figures of a greyish clay. The experiments which he made were in but few instances successful, in consequence of the clay not being adapted to adhere properly to the glass. It was, however, from the Bohemian that the idea was caught by some French manufacturers, who, after having expended a considerable sum in the attempt,

at length succeeded in incrusting several medallions of Buonaparte, which were sold at an enormous price. From the extreme difficulty of making these medallions, and their almost invariably breaking while under the operation of cutting, very few were finished; and the manufacture was upon the point of being abandoned, when it was fortunately taken up by a French gentleman, who, with a perseverance not less honourable to himself, than in its results advantageous to the arts, prosecuted a series of experiments, by which, in a few years, he brought the invention to a state of great

improvement. The French have never succeeded, however, in introducing it into articles of any size, such as decanters, jugs, or plates; but have contented themselves with ornamenting: smelling-bottles

and small trinkets: nor had the invention been applied to heraldry or any other useful purpose, antecedently to the recent improvements upon the art in this country.

"England has always been famed for bringing to perfection, and directing to a useful application, the crude inventions of other countries. A patent has recently been taken out for ornamental incrustations, called *crystallo ceramic*, which bids fair to form an era in the art of glass-making. By the improved process, ornaments of any description, arms, cyphers, portraits, and landscapes, of any variety of colour, may be introduced into the glass, so as to become perfectly imperishable. The substance of which they are composed is *less fusible* than glass, incapable of generating air, and at the same time susceptible of contraction or expansion, as, in the course of manufacture, the glass becomes hot or cold. It may previously be formed into any device or figure by either moulding or modelling; and may be painted with metallic colours, which are fixed by exposure to a melting heat. The ornaments are introduced into the body of the glass *while hot*, by which means the air is effectually excluded, the composition being actually incorporated with the glass. In this way every description of ornamental glass ware may be decorated with embossed white or coloured arms or crests. Specimens of these incrustations have been exhibited, not only in decanters and wine-glasses, but in lamps, girandoles, chimney ornaments, plates, and smelling-bottles. Busts and statues on a small scale, caryatides to support lamps or clocks, masks after the antique, have been introduced with admirable effect.

"The composition used in the patent incrustations is of a silvery appearance, which has a superb effect when introduced into richly cut glass. Miniatures, however, may be enamelled upon it, without the colours losing any of their brilliancy; and thus, instead of being painted on the surface of the crystal, may be embodied in it.

"A most important advantage to bederived from this elegant invention, respects the preservation of inscriptions. Casts of medals and coins present no equal security for perpetuating them. The inscription, when once incrusted in a solid block of crystal, like the fly in amber, will effectually resist for ages the destructive action of the atmosphere.

"It is probable, however, that a collateral advantage of no small importance will result from the invention, inasmuch as it will tend very considerably to enhance the value of British glass wares, and to extend the application of glass to new purposes of domestic utility. The highly ornamental effect which may by this means be given to glass, will recommend these incrustations, in the place of metallic ornaments, for door-plates or handles, bell-pulls, and the inlaid work of tables, looking-glasses, and other sorts of furniture, besides plateaus, and the decorations of the table or side-board. The extension of any branch of national industry at the present time is a consideration of the greatest moment.

"Nor will the invention be considered as wholly unimportant as connected with the progress of the arts. Whatever serves to connect more intimately the ornamental with the useful, has obviously a beneficial operation, more or less directly, on the fine arts. Glass-making itself, though not entitled to that high appellation, is an art, the progress of which cannot but be viewed with interest. It is curious to trace its history from Egypt and Tyre to Rome, thence to Venice, and subsequently to Bohemia, till at last it has attained its perfection in that land 'renowned for arts and arms,' which has eclipsed the maritime greatness of the Syrian city and the Italian state, and become to the moral world, what Egypt and Rome were successively to the world of letters — the focus and the centre."

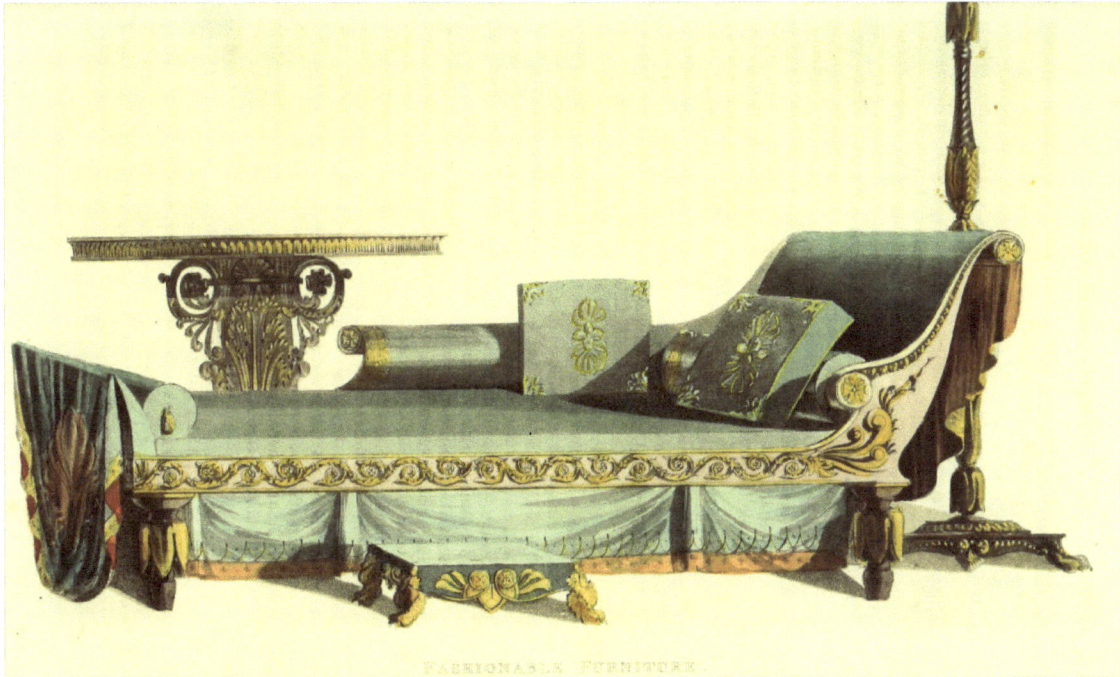

A Sofa, Sofa-Table, Candelabra, and Footstool
February 1822

A SOFA, SOFA-TABLE, CANDELABRA, AND FOOTSTOOL

The picturesque design which is the subject of the annexed plate will afford ample material to a judicious upholsterer for as many articles of furniture as are there represented, and he could not fail to produce examples that would admit an equally pleasing combination.

Although they are the suggestions of an artist unpractised in fabricating such works, and consequently untrammeled by mechanical laws of workmanship and construction, they are admirably suited to executive adoption, with the advantage of scientific and artist-like arrangement of form, ornament, and colours.

The designs are of the highest class of furniture, and should therefore have the richest style of decoration by silk or velvet draperies; and as they are now so admirably produced by the British loom, their employment would aid the advancement of native art, and benefit the country.

The carved work should be splendidly gilt in matted, sanded, and burnished gold; the furniture, delicate green, of a uniform or mixed colours, and the sub-draperies of a colour in which a red tone shall predominate, being those which form harmonies of contrast.

Plate II. Vol. XIII

Secretaire Bookcase
April 1822

SECRETAIRE BOOKCASE

The French artists have been very happy in their contrivance of these elegant pieces of furniture, which they decorate with truly admirable fancy and delicate workmanship. Their modellers draw well in outline, and their chasers have a tact at forming tools suited to small ornaments in metal, not possessed by workmen of any other country employed in the manufacture of light articles of furniture: hence the profusion of small *appliquet* enrichments so prevalent in their designs, and which they diversify into numberless patterns by changes of the several parts, often producing graceful novelties and suggestions for other works.

The annexed design is after the style so exquisitely perfected by M. Persée, the French architect to Buonaparte: it consists of every requisite for a writing-apparatus, inclosed by a flexible shield; the upper and lower compartments being prepared for the reception of books. It forms altogether an elegant piece of furniture for a highly finished *boudoir*.

The English style for such furniture is, however, more simply chaste, and thence perhaps less liable to be affected by changes of fashion. The harmonies of colour and decorative effect of these, particularly as they have lately been introduced by Messrs. Snell of Albemarle- street, are very pleasing, and suited alike to the library, *boudoir*, or drawing-room: indeed the English style of furniture has advanced so rapidly into reputation during the last ten years, that the French themselves have now adopted a large portion of its characteristic richness and simplicity.

A Cloak-Stand and Flower-Stand
July 1822

A CLOAK-STAND AND FLOWER-STAND

The annexed plate represents a clock-stand and flower-stand suited to a small Gothic hall. The former is simple in its construction, and adapted to receive sticks and umbrellas, by having holes in the upper circle; while the lower has rim to contain water that my cumulate from wet umbrellas. It may perhaps be render more convenience by having another row of pegs at the top. The flower-stand forms an elegant piece of furniture in oak, with bronze ornaments, the top being calculated to receive large drooping plants, and a lamp, or glass with gold fish: either say, as a whole, it is perfect in its form, and will be found to add much beauty of a small entrance-hall.

A Flower-Font
August 1822

A FLOWER-FONT

Receptacles for displaying flowers in the chief apartments of well furnished dwellings are always in request, and they admit an infinite variety of form and decoration, from the simplest *monopede* to the most magnificent assemblage of stages. The present design, after a French example, is suited to a drawing-room or *boudoir*, being executed in choice woods and or-molu; in which case the reservoir should be lined with thin milled lead, to contain water, over which a silver net-work should be placed in a rounding form, to support the flowers, and display them to advantage: from the reservoir a pipe should be affixed, so that it may be readily emptied, otherwise the stagnant water and decaying vegetable matters speedily become offensive for want of change.

Flowers admirably harmonize with glass; and if in the present design all the receptacles were made in that material, beautifully cut in the splendid fashion now in use, the design would be very ornamental, and one in each corner of a drawing-room might be well displayed, particularly if constructed as a tripod.

Many such articles of furniture have been executed lately by Blades of Ludgate-hill, the sumptuous effect of which has given an impulse to the glass-manufactures of this country for bold and massive articles, hitherto unknown to its artificers and the public.

A Secretaire Bookcase
September 1822

A SECRETAIRE BOOKCASE

The convenience of a table that shall contain the implements for writing and proper receptacles for papers, is always desirable by the chief of a family, particularly if it can be closed and rendered secure in a very short space of time; and many devices have been resorted to for the purpose of rendering this piece of furniture complete. The annexed design, drawn from a specimen executed by Messrs. Durham, late Morgan, Catherine-street, Strand, is perhaps the best of its kind. It is furnished with every requisite in a very limited compass, and by one operation of the hand, the whole apparatus is either opened or shut, and so that the conveniences for writing are properly placed on the instant, and the paper-bins exposed to view; or as readily every part is closed, and secured by a single lock.

The drawing is made to represent the entire construction of the table, and expose the means used to perform all the objects, as well as to display the general effect of this useful piece of furniture.

It is executed in mahogany, and prepared to admit a greater or less quantity of embellishment, according as the demand may make simplicity or splendour desirable.

Sideboard and Cellaret
October 1822

SIDEBOARD AND CELLARET

The engraving which accompanies this article represents a sideboard and cellaret, suitable for the mansions of the great and opulent. The sideboard is of richly marked mahogany, inlaid with bronze, which may, according to taste, or to suit the dining-room furniture, be more or less so. The head is of an elegant Grecian form, and should be carved from a piece of wood that has but few markings, that the workmanship may shew to advantage. Chairs to accompany this piece of furniture should have backs with a scroll of a similar form. The cellaret is a handsome piece of furniture, and suitable to the sideboard, with apposite ornaments: that of the grapes may be of bronze or carved in mahogany.

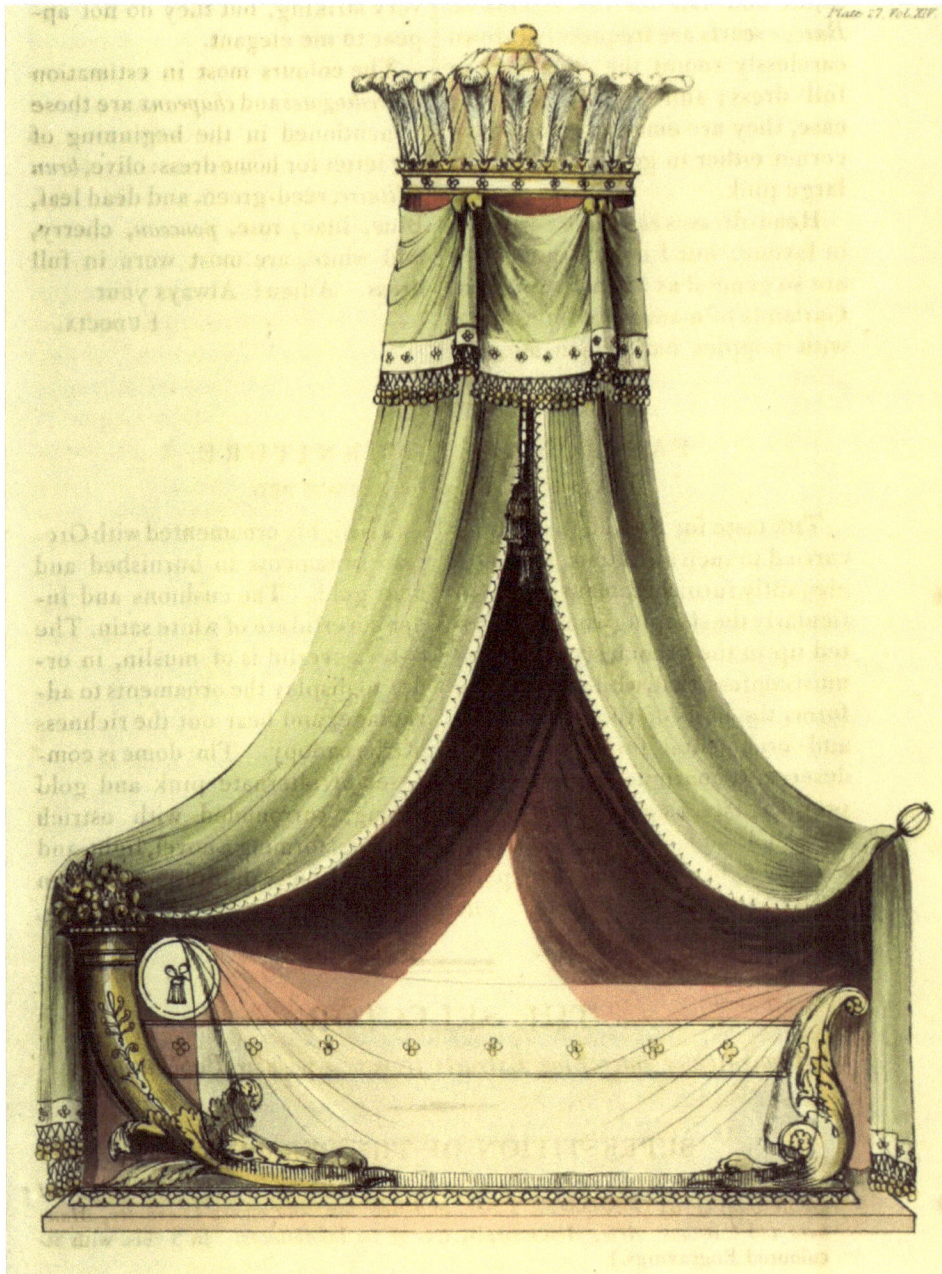

A Sofa, Or French Bed
November 1822

A SOFA, OR FRENCH BED

The taste for French furniture is carried to such an extent, that most elegantly furnished mansions, particularly the sleeping-rooms, are fitted up in the French style; and we must confess, that, while the antique forms the basis of their decorative and ornamental furniture, it will deservedly continue in repute. Our present plate, a sofa, or French bed, designed and decorated in the French style, is adapted for apartments of superior elegance. The sofa is highly ornamented with Grecian ornaments in burnished and matt gold. The cushions and inner coverlid are of white satin. The outer coverlid is of muslin, in order to display the ornaments to advantage, and bear out the richness of the canopy. The dome is composed of alternate pink and gold fluting, surrounded with ostrich feathers, forming a novel, light, and elegant effect: the drapery is green satin, with a salmon-coloured lining.

20

An Egyptian Chimney-Front
December 1822

AN EGYPTIAN CHIMNEY-FRONT

The propriety of designing every piece of furniture so as to correspond with the style of the apartment for which it is destined, has frequently been urged in the course of this publication; and its advantages are now generally admitted, because the public taste is prepared to distinguish the characteristic and leading features of the several styles of art usually adopted in this country; and the eye of taste is offended when articles of furniture are brought together that have not been designed on uniform principles.

In the subject of the annexed plate there are four articles that were not unfrequently placed together, as accident might produce the assemblage: the chimney-piece was bought at the mason's — the grate at the smith's — the frame at the carver's — and the clock, any where so that it was from Paris — all ready-made, all differing in style, and all unlike in composition and execution. Instead of this *melange* of conflicting parts, a uniform whole is now studied, and propriety and suitableness established in its place.

The en graving represents a chimney-piece of Mona marble, or verd antique, and decorated in the Egyptian style. The grate is designed to correspond; and the clock and glass frame are also in a similar style of art, exhibiting at once the advantage of designing every article with reference to the whole and to each other.

21

Ladies' Work-Table
February 1823

LADIES' WORK-TABLE

This elegant table forms a pleasing and commodious appendage to the sitting-room of mansions fitted up in a style of superior elegance. It is equally adapted to the boudoir and drawing-room, and answers the purpose of a drawing- table as well as a work-table, and a desk for writing and reading. The silk bag suspended from the desk is, in the engraving, of azure blue, with silk fringe of the same colour, but should be made to correspond with the colour of the apartment for which the table is designed. In order that it may harmonize with the rest of the furniture, the frame-work should be formed of rose-wood of a rich dark colour, and varied in its grain. The ornaments are wholly of burnished and mat gold.

The top of the table should be adorned with some rich design in water-colours, highly varnished, for the purpose of preserving it: this will be at all times a pleasing object to the eye. Fruit or flowers, well grouped, are particularly to be recommended. The interior may exhibit some pleasing landscape, or any other similar embellishment, according to the taste or fancy of the fair proprietor.

Cabinet Bookcase
May 1823

CABINET BOOKCASE

This elegant piece of furniture forms a useful appendage to the boudoir or drawing-room. It is calculated to contain all the books that may be desired for the sitting-room, without a reference to the library. The doors may be wrought as represented in the design, or in a rich open metal scroll, shewing a coloured silk within; or they may be composed of a chaste lattice-work, with glass, to display the books, which, in this instance, should be elegantly bound, to add richness to the whole. This cabinet should be formed of a deep-toned wood, varied and rich in its grain: rose-wood is preferred. The ornaments are metal gilt. The top is formed in shelves, and lined with looking-glass, to display vases, or any fancy articles that may be required, or that will add to the splendour of the apartment.

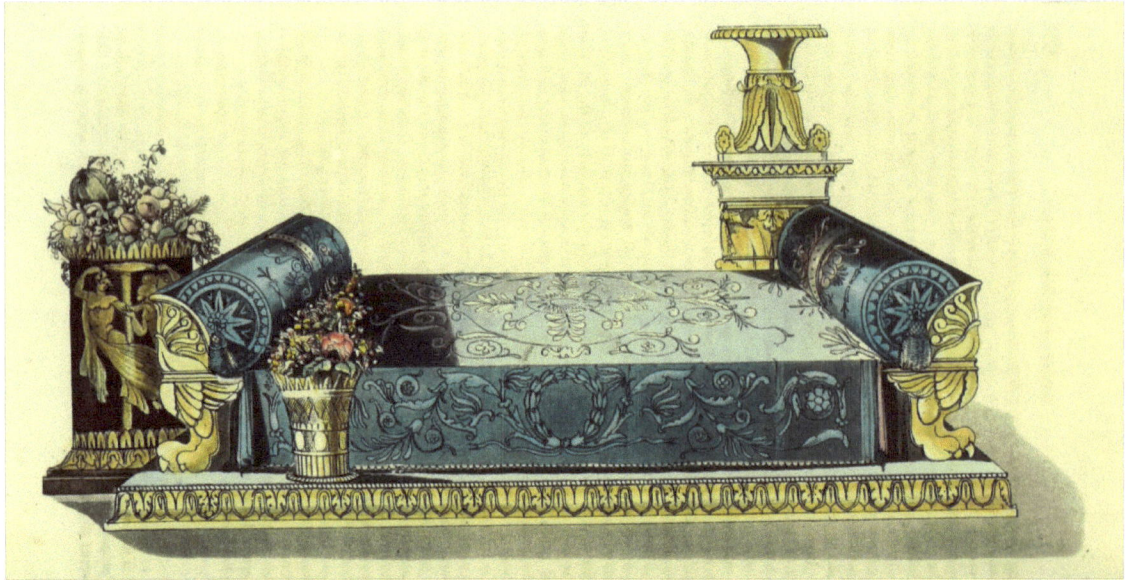

A Faineante and Accompaniments
June 1823

A FAINEANTE AND ACCOMPANIMENTS

The annexed designs are from Parisian models of the respective pieces of furniture, the chief of which is called a *fainéante*, or idler. It is usually placed in the middle of the drawing-room, and about it every kind of decorative article is placed. Here also the *tablette*, the *table de marbre*, and the candelabra, find places, and are interspersed with ottoman-like seats.

The *fainéante* is usually elevated on a platform, as here represented, covered with cloth, the same colour as the silk, satin, or velvet, of which the article itself is composed. This is usually in two colours of the same kind, as dark blue for the ground, and a lighter one for the pattern, and so of any other colour: but in large and splendid apartments, the scroll foliages are frequently embroidered in gold, or of colours that richly and decidedly contrast with the groundwork; and in proportion to the size of the room, so is the magnitude of the *fainéante* increased. The frame-work is composed of rose-wood, satin-wood, or ebony; or is carved and richly gilt: the latter is preferred when the covings are much embellished.

This piece of furniture is suited to the manners of the French; it is a substitute for the fire-place with us, as it becomes the rallying point or conversational centre: here the lady of the mansion seats herself, and here receives her friends; they assemble round her, and thus the party is collected into a group, occupying the middle of the apartment.

Chairs
July 1823

CHAIRS

The annexed plate represents three varieties of chairs, designed for apartments in the first style of elegance. The middle chair is intended for the boudoir, for which it would form an elegant appendage: it is highly wrought in all its parts, and requires to be carefully finished. The frame should be burnished gold. The seat and back are formed of richly figured light blue silk. Persian fringe is suspended from the seat and from the top of the back, while the front is finished with broad gold lace. The chair to the left of the above is intended for the drawing-room: it is an elegant Grecian form: the wood-work is richly finished in burnished and matt gold; the seat and back of green velvet, relieved with a blue or black band. Rich figured silk may be substituted, of a colour to suit the drapery of the room. The third chair is of mahogany, and designed for the parlour: the ornaments are carved in the same wood as the frame of the chair; the legs are turned and beaded: the continued lines on the frame should also be beaded. The seat is covered with red morocco leather, which, combined with the colour of the wood, produces a warm and rich appearance.

A State Bed
September 1823

A STATE BED

   The authors who have written on the arrangement of furniture in *olden* times, have given to the common bed a width of six feet, and to state ones an altitude quite unknown to the present day, except as we see it exemplified in some of our very ancient mansions, whose chambers exhibit the four-post bedstead at from 20 to 30 feet in height. This stateliness, or rather the excess of it, proved, in later times, a complete bar to the occupation of these sumptuous dormitories, and consequently led to the introduction of more compact and accessible, if not more graceful and imposing, pieces of furniture.

   The present design exhibits a modern bedstead, and furniture decorated with Gothic ornaments, and with draperies woven to assimilate with them. The canopy of a throne, or rather that which in sumptuous processions was borne over the chief in honour, was the precursor of the English tester; and in the annexed engraving, the original has been reverted to for the embellishments of its cornice, and the draperies suspended from them; and the coverlet and the head-draperies are after the rich tissues and tapestries that usually accompanied this species of ornamental parade.

   The recurrence to such sources for designs of furniture for buildings in the Gothic style is to be desired, because they afford the means of assimilating them to such edifices, in accordance with the practices of the times which they are intended to imitate.

A Study Bookcase and Medal Cabinet
January 1824

A STUDY BOOKCASE AND MEDAL CABINET

It is proposed to introduce to our readers, through the present year, a Series of new Examples of Furniture, that may not only be useful as single articles, but may benefit the general manufacture, as they will be designed, on correct principles, and frequently in combination with the proper decoration of the apartments to which they are suited, and in connection with useful accompaniments.

When due regard is paid to the proportions of the relative parts in such an article of furniture as is exhibited in the annexed plate, it cannot fail to please; and when executed in suitable materials, and decorated with propriety, it becomes an ornamental appendage, not inferior to the demands of the most finished library, and for which purpose it was made; but more expressly intended for the reception of gems, medals, and minerals, than for books merely; and also for portfolios of drawings, prints, and such objects of study which are not usually provided for in bookcases ; and it is so arranged as to form a complete piece of furniture for the end of a room, or, on the side, become a central object between bookcases.

The manufacturer will immediately perceive that the parts are capable of separation, and that he may form from them several handsome pieces of furniture, according as an apartment may need variety of form and quantity.

Glass doors may be substituted for those of the design, where book-bindings are to be displayed; but in general, curtains of cloth or silk, or of other coloured materials, are more ornamental, and more readily made to harmonize with the wood-work.

The manufacture of British woods, such as the pollard oak and elm, cut transversely near the roots, is now so well understood, and so beautiful when thus applied, that they need no other recommendation to the admirers of superior furniture.

A Cabinet Dressing-Case
February 1824

A CABINET DRESSING-CASE

The annexed plate represents an elegant cabinet dressing-case: it is formed of fine mahogany, and richly carved. The lower part incloses a drawer, with wash-bason, ewer, &c. complete. The upper part contains three mirrors, in sliding frames and running on centres, with sundry divisions and cases for small and large bottles; the whole forming an ornamental and useful piece of furniture, suitable for a dressing or sitting-room.

We have been kindly permitted by Mr. Durham to copy this handsome piece of furniture at his manufactory, 26, Catherine-street, Strand.

A French Bed and Decoration of the Chamber
March 1824

A FRENCH BED AND DECORATION OF THE CHAMBER

The end of the apartment being sufficiently recessed to receive the tripod supports of the drapery, they stand in the situation represented in the annexed plate during the day-time, but at night they may be drawn forward with the curtains, so as to canopy the bed in as ample a manner as may be desired, and thus obtain a larger inclosure than is usual with this article of furniture. The bed itself is prepared to draw forward on rollers, either accompanied by the semicircular back or otherwise, as by a simple means it is readily attached or liberated.

The colour of the apartment being a light blue, the draperies would harmonize if of a delicate fawn or pink, lined with white. The basket is intended to contain artificial flowers, and each tripod would be decorated in a similar manner. The chairs and other furniture should be designed in a corresponding style.

A Cabinet Glass
April 1824

A CABINET GLASS

This piece of furniture is intended for a cabinet room, the chief parts of which are supposed to be fitted up with receptacles for medals, coins, gems, and also for collections in conchology, entomology, and other specimens in natural history. The glass frame is suitably designed, and composed of similar materials to the cabinet, and is intended to combine with the general fittings-up of the apartment. If executed in satin wood, or in stained imitations of it, it would have a pleasing effect; and the chairs and tables being designed to correspond, the whole would be considerably improved. Lilac, bright green, and fawn colours agree admirably for the wall - colours and draperies of rooms so fitted up, which should have the appearance of study and retirement.

Astronomical Clock
May 1824

ASTRONOMICAL CLOCK

The clock represented in our engraving, of a new and elegant shape, 13 inches in diameter and 25 in height, stands covered with a glass bell upon a handsome pedestal about 3 feet high, the whole forming a very useful and tasteful ornament for a drawing-room or library.

The merit of the invention consists in its combining and exhibiting at one view the state of the world, as acted upon in the progress of time by the diurnal and annual revolution of the heavenly bodies immediately connected with our globe, according to the Copernican system; shewing, at the same time, the hours and the corresponding position of those bodies in their respective orbits. This result is obtained as follows :

To the clock is annexed a complicated, and at the same time a simply and beautifully executed kind of orrery, which is put in motion by the clock, and as they perform together their several motions, they shew —

1. The division of the hour; 2. The hour of the day; 3. The day of the week; 4. The day of the month; 5. The month of the year; 6. The degree and sign of the zodiac; 7. The diurnal rotation of the earth upon its axis, producing the alternations of day and night for the different countries of the globe; 8. The gradual progress of the earth in its annual revolution round the sun, combined with its elliptical movement, which causes it to approach to, and recede from, the sun according to the seasons; 9. The diurnal and annual rotation and elliptical motion of the moon round the earth as its satellite, with its phases, indicating at the same time its age; and, 10. By means of a revolving dial placed above the globe, the true time, and also (at will) the hour of the day or night, in any given part of the world.

31

ASTRONOMICAL CLOCK - Continued

To add to the utility of this invention, it is so contrived that, by slightly altering the position of a single wheel, the orrery is rendered independent of the clock, and may then be put in motion with any degree of celerity by a handle, for the purpose of demonstration, as long and as often as it is found necessary or thought proper; after which it is sufficient to give to the handle a retrograde motion, until the hand of the zodiac-dial is brought back to the proper day of the month, and to replace the connecting wheel, in order to re-establish the action of the clock upon the orrery as before.

Taken thus singly, the orrery will be found to give a most satisfactory practical illustration of the elements of cosmography and geography, by rendering perceptible those motions which, in their joint operation with the clock, are too slow to be sensible to the eye.

The progression of the common and leap year points out the period at which the orrery must be wound up, which occurs only once in four years.

The ingenuity and utility of this contrivance reflect great credit on the skill of the inventor, Mr. Raingo, watchmaker, of Paris, who has obtained a patent from the French government for the manufacture of it.

Drawing-Room Table, Chairs, and Footstools
June 1824

DRAWING-ROOM TABLE, CHAIRS, AND FOOTSTOOLS

These articles of furniture are proposed to be executed in rose-wood, and partially gilt; or the ornamental work carved in satin-wood; both of which have a very rich and decorative effect. The coverings of the seats are of stamped velvet or of silk, and the backs may properly be stuffed and covered also. The furniture executed by the late Mr. G. Bullock was of this character and style, and it is continued with much taste by the chief upholsterers of the day.

The tables generally used are round, and of oblong forms, a little carved at the ends.

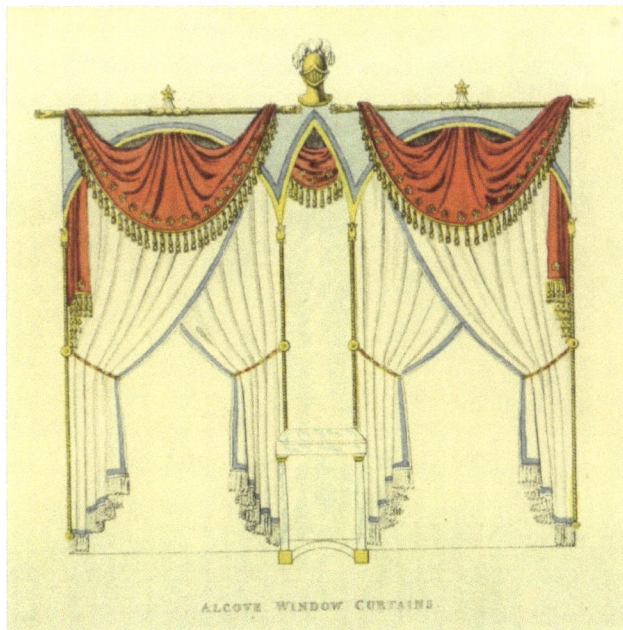

Alcove Window-Curtains
July 1824

ALCOVE WINDOW-CURTAINS

The annexed design is intended to assimilate with the decoration of an apartment, in which the walls are formed into arches, and coloured in corresponding blue tints. The arches of the curtains are formed by fine cloth strained on brass rods, which project so much as to receive the draperies, and to conceal the curtain-laths, &c. The transparent hangings are looped to the supporting rods, and the festoons are thrown over the upper poles. This is altogether a new arrangement, and has a very agreeable effect when executed.

Drawing-Room Sofa
September 1824

DRAWING-ROOM SOFA

The frame of this sofa should be made of fine rose-wood richly covered, the raised parts of which would have a good effect if relieved with burnished gold. The scrolls being inverted, form an easy and elegant support for the pillows: the back is a little reclined, to receive pillows also; all of which should be covered in the prevailing taste with silk or Merino damask, trimmed with silk cords and tassels.

We are indebted for this design to a drawing executed by Mr. John Taylor, upholsterer, Bedford-court, Covent-Garden.

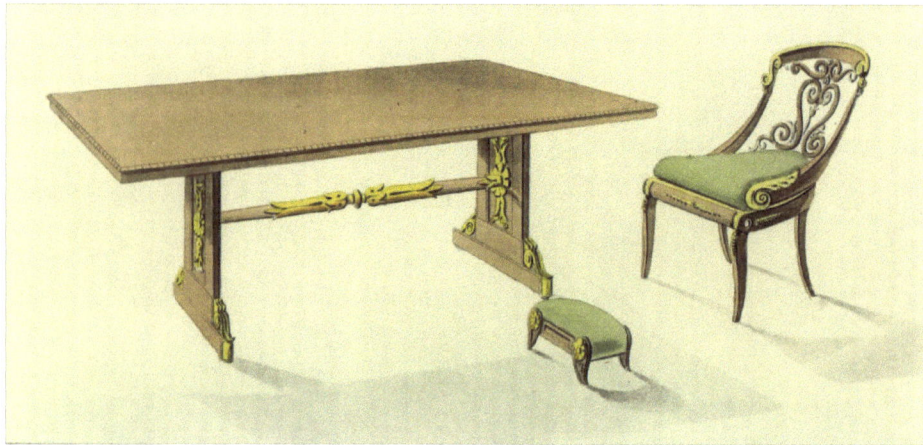

Sofa-Table, Chair, and Footstool
October 1824

SOFA-TABLE, CHAIR, AND FOOTSTOOL

The table is of rose-wood, relieved by carved ornaments in satin-wood, and is of very simple construction, although of adequate strength. The chair is composed of the same materials, and the cushion supposed to be covered with merino damask. The form of the back produces a very agreeable support to the person seated; and in effect the whole, if well carved, is rich, and perfectly suited to harmonize with the best furniture of the drawing-room.

The footstool is designed in a corresponding style. The delicacy of the workmanship necessary to the full effect of furniture designed in this manner makes it costly; but those who possess it have the benefit of knowing that it will never become common-place, and from its artist like merits will always be valuable.

Two Designs for Chairs
November 1824

TWO DESIGNS FOR CHAIRS

The first is intended as a library chair; and would have a good effect if executed in oak, with pillow-cushion covered with fine crimson cloth, and tufts of the same colour: the back is intended to be a little hollow, and stuffed in unison with the seat-cushion.

The other, on the right, is an elegant design for a drawing-room chair; and would look extremely handsome if executed in white and gold; or if this was thought too delicate, zebra wood, relieved with burnished gold, would have a good effect: the seat covered with damask or satin, with an appropriate gimp, &c.

We are indebted for these designs to drawings executed by Mr. John Taylor, upholsterer, Bedford-court, Covent-Garden.

Sofa, Candelabrum, Table, and Footstool
February 1825

SOFA, CANDELABRUM, TABLE, AND FOOTSTOOL

These examples are intended as the furniture of a *boudoir* or lady's dressing-room. The covering and draperies of the sofa are of silk, and the frame-work and carving of yellow satin-wood, the parts being heightened by burnished gilding. The foot-stool is of corresponding design and manufacture; and the table is supposed to be formed in Java wood, and relieved by ornamental inlayings, to correspond with the couch.

The candelabrum is intended as a support for flowers, a glass globe for fish, or to receive a pastille-frame.

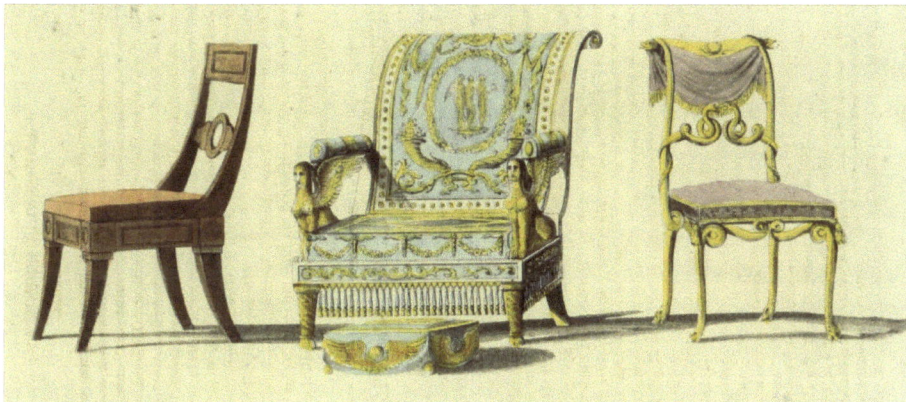

Designs for Chairs
March 1825

DESIGNS FOR CHAIRS

The shape of the dining-room chair is well known to form a very agreeable seat; it stands very firmly, and is of a superior class of furniture: it should be executed in mahogany, and finished with the varnish called French polish. This gives considerable brilliance to the wood, preserves its colour, and is benefited by use.

The central chair is very much carved, and should be finished in dead white and gold. The covering is of British satin, in which the looms of the country are so successful at the present time, and embellished with ornamental devices in gold colours on a light blue ground. This design reminds the spectator of the splendid furniture lately executed for his Grace the Duke of Northumberland by Messrs. Morell and Hughes. The footstool is of similar materials.

The last design is for the chair of a boudoir, and is composed of snake-like forms in burnished gold: the seat-covering and festoon-drapery are of satin.

35

A Sideboard
April 1825

A SIDEBOARD

The proportion necessary to a sideboard, its general form and magnitude, render this article of furniture highly useful in the decoration of a dining-room: it has accordingly received from time to time a careful attention. The artist has sometimes bestowed upon it the result of his studies amongst the works of the

Greeks and Romans, by which his designs have become classical and imposing; and this has given to furniture a corresponding value amongst men of taste, who perceive, that the operations of the mind can be identified with the labours of the tablemaker, and that each piece of furniture may become a source of delightful contemplation.

The annexed plate represents a sideboard of this order of furniture: the Chimeras that support it are from a fine example of antiquity, and capable of producing a bold and varied effect, as shewn by the end view which accompanies the elevation.

In general, it should be executed in mahogany, and highly polished: if the wood be of superior quality, it would be very handsome; but for a sumptuous apartment, the ornaments might properly be gilded.

36

Table, Chair, and Window-Seat
May 1825

TABLE, CHAIR, AND WINDOW-SEAT

These examples of modern French furniture will be acceptable to our subscribers, as they present a novelty, arising from the introduction of metal -work to obtain an effect of lightness, by making those parts open and delicate that have lately been the most solid of the several articles. That style is quite departed from in these designs, which makes the ornamental portions of them merely *applique*; for the table is supported by a tripod of dolphins, without the aid of a stem, as usually introduced in the lately prevailing manner; and the decorations of the chair are chiefly relieved by perforations, instead of a solid ground-work.

The table may be executed in any of the ornamental woods: the dolphins are supposed to be in bronze, and the feet in or-molu.

The chair is of white and gold, with a satin seat; and the settee is covered to correspond, and finished with gold lace and fringes.

GOTHIC FIRE PLACE.

A Gothic Chimney-Piece and Stove
June 1825

A GOTHIC CHIMNEY-PIECE AND STOVE

The prevailing taste for Gothic architecture renders valuable every information that may be collected towards assisting the artisan in perfecting his works; and for this purpose the design is here introduced.

It is of considerable importance, where several manufacturers are engaged in forming a whole, as in the present instance, that they should all perceive the relative connection that the several parts ought to have with each other: thus, from the annexed design, the statuary (so called merely because he works marble of which sculptors make statues,) will form the chimney-piece, so as to receive gracefully the works of the sculptor destined to adorn the tabernacles in the design. The smith will perceive the necessity of making his stove conformable to the peculiarity of style; the maker of the fender and its accessories will also follow the example; and all unite in obtaining an effect of propriety, and which propriety is an object of the first importance to architectural beauty. But to enable these different manufacturers to produce this necessary concordance, it is evident that the architect must precede their labours, by laying down a guide in this way for their observance and regulation; for without this first preparation, as many varieties of style may be expected as articles employed, and instead of a uniform whole, a jumble of incongruities, as offensive to the eye as to the judgment.

38

A Camp-Bedstead
July 1825

A CAMP-BEDSTEAD

    The annexed plate is designed to exhibit the manner in which the chief chamber in the house of a military officer may be furnished, and so as to accord with his rank and appointments. The frame-work is of mahogany, and the trophies of war carved and gilt. The bed is supported by inverted mortars at the four corners, and the draperies by groups of swords, spears, &c. and by representations of the graceful swan, all indicative of repose and peace. The star of glory decorates the head-curtain; and the whole design is surmounted by coronets and small statues of Victory and Fame.

    The draperies are of rich lavender-coloured silk, with amber linings, gold lace fringe and tassels.

A Gothic Lantern
August 1825

A GOTHIC LANTERN

Every article that is used as the furniture of a nobleman's mansion is now expected to have the benefit of chaste design, and not, as formerly, to be manufactured according to the crude notions of the mere workman: in fact, there is no trade that will admit of the employment of the artist but he is called upon to exert his talent; and thus the commonest materials are made valuable by the art that is displayed by them; and which will be still more usefully encouraged when the fashion has passed away, so common at present, of making every thing in the old French style of works executed in the reign of Louis XIV.; a style so little amenable to good sense and real taste, that it would rarely meet with patrons if it were not thrust before the public by manufacturers, in consequence of its easy execution and defiance of correct drawing, and by which the clumsiest workman will pass current for an accomplished one.

The annexed design is for a Gothic lantern, intended for the hall of a nobleman, in the same character of architecture; it is intended to contain six Argand lamps. The whole is in lackered brass, and plate glass, each square being twenty inches wide, and fifty inches high.

An Ornamental Air-Stove
September 1825

AN ORNAMENTAL AIR-STOVE

The economy of fuel and the means of ventilating and warming apartments have employed the attention of the scientific for some years; and when, as in the annexed design, these objects, so important to health and comfort, are ingeniously effected without damage to the building wherein the means are employed, and at no greater expense than is the common cost of fitting up fireplaces with stoves and marble chimney-pieces, it may be expected that the benefit it offers will be duly appreciated by the public.

The stove, which in fact is both stove and chimney-piece, and requires no other, is entirely of metal, having suitable retorts at the back, through which the air passes from the apartment, and becomes heated by the fire in the grate; and indeed the stove is altogether an air-chamber, capable of benefiting in a very great degree from every portion of the fire with which it comes in contact.

The present design is quite new, and, in point of elegance, a novelty also in the manufacture of independent stoves. In execution, the brilliancy of the metals of which it is made gives an effect to this piece of furniture that cannot be adequately represented on paper. The drawing was, however, taken from the stove at the manufactory of Messrs. May and Morrit in Oxford-street, to whom we are indebted for permission to insert it in the *Repository of Arts*.

The ground-work, as it is called, is of steel; the ornaments are brass or or-molu: the latter is made to remove easily for the purpose of cleaning, an operation that is exceedingly simple; and the ornamental part is capable of being reapplied by any one in a few minutes.

A Bookcase
October 1825

A BOOKCASE

Towards the latter end of the 14th century and the commencement of the 15th, that style of architecture commonly called Gothic became excessively rich. Every space was fitted up with tracery and ornaments; and though it wanted repose, yet it had such an elegant and picturesque appearance, that it was considered worthy of imitation in the book-case represented in the engraving. Being on a small scale, no kind of turrets are here introduced, but simply four buttresses and pinnacles, with a sort of parapet at the top. The arches are made very flat, which form is considered more appropriate for domestic architecture than the pointed, which seems better calculated for ecclesiastical purposes. A figure, the symbol of Meditation, has been placed at the top, and is supported by a rich bracket. Though coloured glass should be used only where light can be admitted behind, in order to relieve it, still it has a pleasing effect, and gives to the whole a fanciful appearance. This piece of furniture may be made use of for holding other things than books, such as antiquities, &c.

42

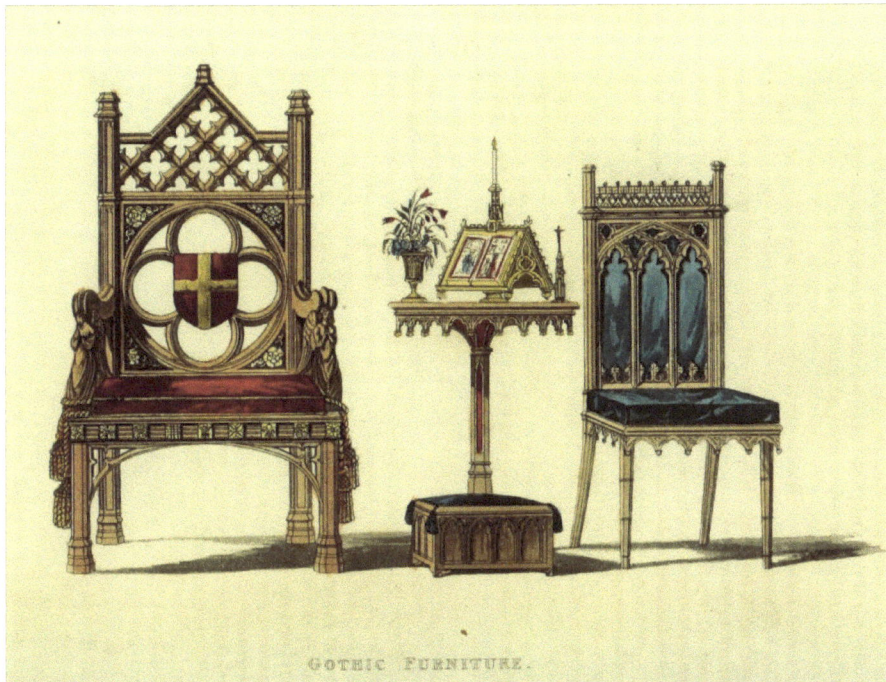

Episcopal Chair
November 1825

EPISCOPAL CHAIR

In the time of Henry VII. and in the early part of the reign of Henry VIII. architecture was peculiar for its lightness and richness of parts, which are well suited for furniture. The style of the annexed chair is of that date, and its parts are chiefly taken from King's College Chapel, Cambridge. The two arms supported by angels are from Henry VIIth's Chapel, Westminster Abbey. In order to preserve unity of character, the wood is of light oak with gilt mouldings, relieved by rich crimson velvet cushions and tassels. This chair may be introduced with propriety into a church, prelate's mansion, or an extensive library. In order to prevent heaviness, the ornaments at top, as well as the quatrefoils, are kept open.

DRAWING-ROOM CHAIR

This specimen may be considered of the florid style. On account of the fulness and richness of its ornaments, and also on account of the flatness of the arch which is introduced in the back, this chair would require a great nicety of execution, the parts being very delicate. The wood is light oak, and the mouldings gilt; the tracery should be filled up with velvet of the same colour as the room: perhaps it would be more appropriate if it were of rose-wood or cedar.

TABLE FOR A BOUDOIR

This table, of a circular form, may be either of oak or of rose-wood. Upon it a reading-desk is introduced in the style of those formerly used in churches: this has been partly taken from one kept in the library on the side of King's College Chapel. An ornament is introduced in the top to receive the light, as also on the side of it an inkstand in the form of a Gothic tower. A missal is here represented, to express that the room is kept chiefly for religious meditations: the word *boudoir* being very indefinite in the French language, gives room to admit of its being adapted particularly to this purpose.

43

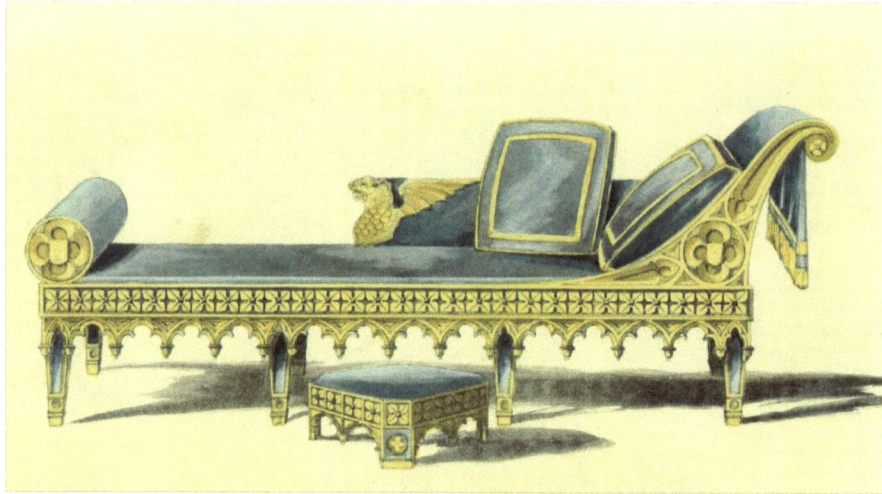

Sofa for a Drawing-Room in the Gothic Style
December 1825

SOFA FOR A DRAWING-ROOM IN THE GOTHIC STYLE

This piece of furniture, in which the modern form is preserved, is embellished according to the style of the 13th century; or rather the parts are adapted from Gothic tracery executed at that period, so as to combine the peculiar features of Gothic art with the form that is now considered to afford the best accommodation for its purpose.

The frame-work may be executed in oak, and partially gilded; or in other materials, and wholly finished in mat and burnished gold: the covering and cushions of velvet or satin. The chairs and other furniture should be corresponding in style of course, and the apartment of the same character, although it may be much more simple in its parts.

The fashion of making the coverings of furniture similar in point of colour to the walls of the room has at length subsided, and the colour now chosen for them is such as will form harmonious combinations: the colour selected should be therefore governed by this circumstance.

44

A Sofa (misprint)
January 1826

A SOFA

   The taste for Gothic architecture is rapidly extending; many of the mansions of our nobility and gentry, recently erected, are in this elegant style, which is not confined to the rich and romantic outline of the exterior, but is equally beautiful within. The furniture forms one of the leading features of the interior decorations: of the different styles of architecture of the middle ages, none seems so well adapted for furniture as the florid, on account of the pleasing variety and minuteness of its parts. The artist is aware that Gothic furniture has been objected to on account of the multiplicity of its angles, which (it is needless to observe) there is no occasion for.

   The subject chosen for the annexed plate is a sofa (misprint), which at once proves the truth of the above assertion. In the present example it will be found that the style of the time of Henry III. has been mixed with that of the 15th century: though the writer is well aware, that unity of character should prevail, he thinks, notwithstanding, that in objects simply of fancy and fashion it may be deviated from, if symmetry and harmony of details are observed. It is almost superfluous to add, that the general colour of the room directs that of the furniture, which should be ornamented with or-moulu or rose-wood.

Published on the second page of the next (February) issue:
   ERRATUM

   In the descriptive article under the head of FASHIONABLE FURNITURE, inserted in our last Number, page 60, the word SOFA in the title, and in the second line of the second column, should be SIDEBOARD.

Gothic Window-Curtain
February 1826

GOTHIC WINDOW-CURTAIN

In the annexed plate is given a representation of an oriel window, well adapted for the termination of a gallery or drawing-room; and as this elegant part of Gothic architecture was never employed in ecclesiastical buildings, it may be introduced with the greatest propriety in modern Gothic houses. But to enable the architect the better to place this decoration, it may not be amiss to enter into a few historical particulars respecting it. It has been supposed, and with very good reason, by men of great antiquarian knowledge and research, that the oriel is derived from the Moorish and Persian styles: they allege that *oriel* means *east*, and that as those nations were worshippers of the sun, they constructed small projecting cabinets, where they might pay their early devotions to that rising luminary. Most certainly it was first introduced in this country as an oratory, or place of prayer; it was then built upon a richly carved bracket projecting from a bed-chamber, and containing just space enough for one or two persons: but in the reigns of Henry the Seventh and Eighth it took a different character, and became the accompaniment of halls and places of festivity, when it was, without exception, built upon the dais, and projected from one of the sides of the building. It was then considered as the place of honour; and in the universities it was the usual seat of the master and as many of the fellows as could conveniently sit within it. By the occasional introduction of stained glass, a most pleasing effect is produced by the rays of the sun; and this will give a cheerful appearance to a room which otherwise might appear gloomy. In fine, it may be considered as one of the great beauties with which the style of architecture of the middle ages is replete.

In the accompanying plate the window takes the whole width of the room, and shews three sides of an octagon; and in order to admit the whole of the light, the curtains are placed at a little distance from it.

It is well known that the brilliant colours and richness of ornament of the fourteenth and fifteenth centuries never were surpassed: it is attempted to be imitated in this design, by introducing velvet curtains, enriched with appropriate ornaments and coloured glass. With the surrounding decorations, it is adapted for a boudoir on the east or south side of a private mansion.

Gothic Library-Table
March 1826

GOTHIC LIBRARY-TABLE

In the accompanying plate is given a representation of a Gothic table, adapted for a library or place of study. As the workmanship of tables is carried to a greater degree of perfection in this country than any other, this specimen it is hoped will be useful to the upholsterer.

Tables indisputably are of great antiquity; those used by the Romans were stone or marble, of which several examples have recently been found in the excavations of Pompeii and Herculaneum. But we may even trace them to higher antiquity, since Moses, in the Book of *Exodus*, chap. xxv. verses 23, 24, 25, mentions the table of show-bread as being made of shittim-wood, overlaid with plates of pure gold.

In the earlier part of the middle ages, from the few examples now remaining, they are supposed to have been constructed in iron; but in the more refined aera of the fourteenth and fifteenth centuries, the materials employed were oak or chesnut-wood, carved with great delicacy and taste. It is from this period that our design has been formed. Beneath the top, the artist has introduced the square quatrefoil, an ornament greatly in vogue at that time, and which forms a pleasing variation to the eye from the usual circular quatrefoil. The griffins to support the base are taken from that most elegant Gothic edifice of the latter end of the fifteenth century, the *Palais de Justice*, at Rouen. The shape of the table is circular; and in this respect it differs from ancient examples, which are generally of the parallelogram shape.

Gothic Bed
April 1826

GOTHIC BED

There is not, perhaps, any piece of furniture which has been more varied in its materials and ornaments, than a bed; though there is no example of its having deviated from a square or parallelogram form; but the canopies are of infinite variety in their shape.

It is not at all surprising that an object which contributes so much to the comfort of mankind should have been so much attended to, and adorned with great richness and taste; and indeed this appears to have been the case even from the most remote antiquity. Respecting the decoration of the beds of the ancients we have little or no information; but, judging from the magnificence of the Greeks and Romans, in their cities, mansions, and dress, we may naturally infer that their beds were very superb.

In the dark ages which immediately followed the fall of the Roman empire, we have but very little account of the manners, customs, and architecture of the barbarians who then inhabited the now enlightened Europe.

The next important era in history, was the conquest of England by William the Norman. The Normans at that period had begun to cultivate the civil arts and sciences, which made such rapid progress in the succeeding centuries; but even then they had but a very rude idea of that luxury which so eminently distinguished the fifteenth and sixteenth centuries; which is proved by a bed recently discovered in a castle near Lynn, Norfolk, supposed to be coeval with the Conquest. It was made of iron, of great solidity and massiveness. We will now turn to the above-mentioned centuries, when the beauty of the florid style shone in its full lustre; when every detail, however small, was finished with the greatest delicacy and taste: it is of this date that we may reckon that superb relic of ancient art, the bed of Richard III. which as a whole is grand, and the details both rich and elegant. This bed may therefore be considered as one of the best models for modern decorations. Those of the Elizabethan era are but bad copies of the Roman style, mixed with Gothic, and therefore not worthy of our imitation.

The present design is of the period which is termed florid: the griffins introduced at the angles are from the monument of Thomas Bouchier, in Westminster Abbey, and the rest of the details are taken from ancient specimens.

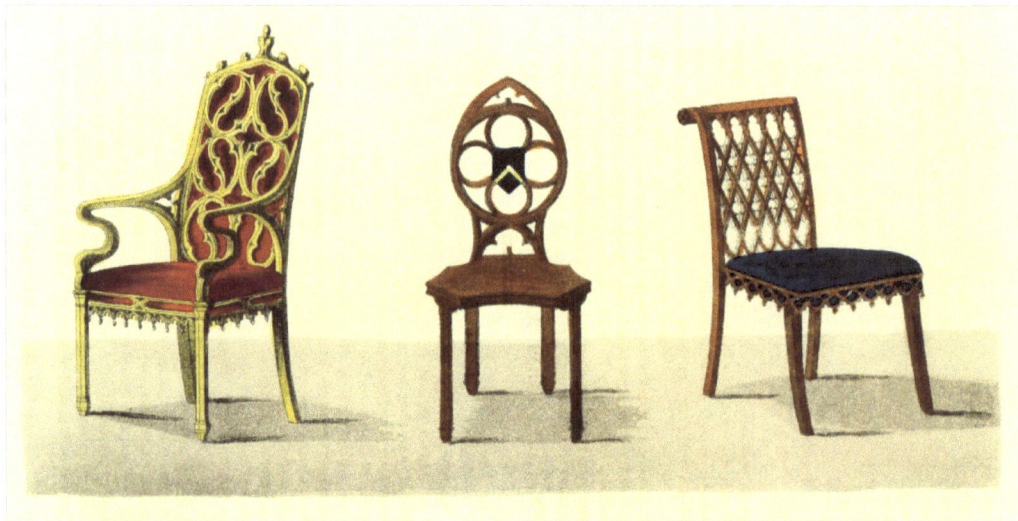

Gothic Chairs
May 1826

GOTHIC CHAIRS

In the annexed plate of Gothic furniture are represented three chairs, one for a hall, and the other two for a drawing-room. It is not, perhaps, generally understood, that it is to a comparatively modern period that we owe the great addition to our domestic comforts derived from this kind of seat. The Romans, at their meals, usually lay in a reclining position on couches; and it is well known that among the Eastern nations no other posture, but that of reclining on cushions or sofas, has ever been practised: it may be, therefore, inferred that it is in Europe this invention took its rise. In England, at so late a period as the reigns of Henry VII. and VIII. chairs appear to have been but very little used ; and it was not till the reign of Queen Elizabeth that they became more generally employed. To this day, in the halls of our universities, the master alone is seated in a chair, the fellows and students being accommodated with forms and benches.

Some of the remaining specimens of ancient chairs are remarkable for the beauty of their design and the richness of their ornaments. Such is that at St. Mary's-Hall, Coventry, which has so justly excited the attention of the curious and the admiration of the decorator. This chair, which is of the style termed florid, is carved in oak, and has a high rising back, which is divided into three panels of tracery, surmounted by two richly carved string - courses. At each end of these rises a sort of bracket, on which are placed the armorial bearings of the person for whom the chair was designed. The seat-part is supported by tracery, and the elbows are formed by figures on a ridge of oak-leaves, which has a very rich effect; and the whole is designed in an harmonious and agreeable manner. But, while we admire the beauties of this design, we are not insensible to its defects; its massy form renders it much too cumbrous to be moved, and, after the numerous modern improvements that have been made in furniture, it would be folly implicitly to copy the ancient examples; though, at the same time, care may be taken to preserve and introduce those parts of the design which are most suited to our purpose.

We have particularly referred to this specimen, because it is the most deserving of our attention; but besides it there are many other examples, such as the two coronation-chairs in Westminster Abbey, which, though inferior in workmanship and design, have, notwithstanding, a good Gothic character.

GOTHIC CHAIRS – Continued

There is, perhaps, no part of furniture which has required more reflection in its construction than a chair. Having constantly a weight to support, strength was one of the principal considerations; and, at the same time, a certain degree of lightness was requisite to fit it to be easily moved. Curves were, therefore, selected as answering two ends; namely, ease to the body, and strength to support it. It is, therefore, not without great study that this piece of furniture has been brought to the state of perfection in which we now see it. The present designs need no particular illustration; they are composed on the improved principles, with some few decorations to give them a more Gothic character.

Gothic Window-Curtains
June 1826

GOTHIC WINDOW-CURTAINS

The annexed plate represents one side of a small room fitted up in the Gothic style.

There is, perhaps, no part of Gothic decoration which requires more reflection than the interior of a room. Among the few remaining specimens which can convey any idea of the ancient splendour of the interior of rooms, is that of the abbess at the abbey of St. Amand, at Rouen, in Normandy; and even this, elegant as it is, affords but a very slight conception of the luxury of the middle ages. The decorator must, therefore, consult ecclesiastical architecture. But here a new difficulty occurs; which is, that were he to take the arrangement of a whole, and to adapt it to the space of almost any apartment, it would appear more like the model of part of a building, than an architectural composition; and, on the other hand, were he to place the details in their real proportion, they would appear large and over-powering; and it is that medium and beauty of proportion, so difficult to attain, which alone is pleasing to the eye.

Curtains, although not an architectural ornament, form, nevertheless, a very essential part of interior decoration. The various arrangements of which they are susceptible, the pliancy of their forms, and the different effects that may be produced by their combinations, render them peculiarly useful to the decorator. Of late, the curtain-rod, as in the present design, has been continued the whole length of the room, and, in this instance, passes behind a Gothic ornament. The curtain pins are also in unison with it.

Horizontal Grand Piano-Forte
July 1826

HORIZONTAL GRAND PIANO-FORTE

The knowledge of music is now so generally diffused, that musical instruments are almost become an essential part of furniture, and among them we can reckon none more frequently used than the piano: we have, therefore, selected it for the subject of the annexed plate, which represents a horizontal grand piano-forte. As this, from its size, would be a leading feature in any apartment, it ought to partake of the style of decoration adopted for the latter.

This instrument being totally unknown to our ancestors, and only invented within the last half century, we can merely decorate the given forms by traceries and other Gothic ornaments best calculated to assist the sound, and to fulfil the intent of the instrument. We have chosen the style of the 15th century, as being the most applicable to our purpose, and admitting the greatest variety of arrangement.

The stool partakes also of the same character.

The appellation *piano -forte* is compounded of two Italian words, which signify *soft* and *loud*, intimating that this instrument can be played in either manner; and in this respect it differs from the harpsichord, which is not capable of that variation.

Flower-Stands
August 1826

FLOWER-STANDS

Among the various decorations of modern apartments we can reckon none, perhaps, more pleasing than a flower-stand: it diversifies and enlivens the appearance of almost any room; and the odoriferous perfume proceeding from the flowers, and the beautiful appearance of their variegated hues, tend at once to delight and charm the senses. There is no style more appropriate for this sort of decoration than the Gothic: its crockets, finials, foliage, pendants, &c. all flowing and pliable, seem to be a continuation of nature; while its open and fanciful traceries contribute to the lightness of its effect.

Whether the flower-stand is of any great antiquity or not, we cannot pretend to determine; but of this we are certain, that if of modern introduction, it is one of the greatest improvements in the decorative style, and is now almost universally adopted. But different situations have been assigned to flower-stands in apartments; some place them in the windows, others in niches or recesses; and, indeed, their position is regulated entirely by taste.

It is hoped that the designs in the annexed plate will, in some sort, exemplify our observation, that Gothic is the most appropriate style for this sort of decoration. Two different designs are given; they are both square in their plan, and may be executed either in fancy wood or metal.

Candelabra
September 1826

CANDELABRA

If the merit of the invention of candelabra is due to the Greeks, the Romans are certainly entitled to great praise for the perfection to which they brought this kind of decoration, most elaborate and beautiful specimens of which have been discovered, not only in the excavations of Pompeii, but in other parts of Italy.

They are generally either of bronze or marble, and their richness corresponds with the magnificent character of the Roman architecture. This sort of decoration seems not to have been employed in the middle ages; indeed there is no record by which we can form any certain criterion to judge of the manner of lighting apartments at that period. The most probable conjecture is, that as candles were so much used in the religious ceremonies, they were also introduced for other purposes. In many cases, perhaps, the only light diffused through the apartment proceeded from either a blazing fire or firsplinters; and to this very day in some northern countries this latter method is still practised.

At the time when the Roman style of architecture was adopted in this country, candelabra were also introduced, and have since formed a conspicuous part of elegant furniture. We now employ them in halls, staircases, libraries, and even drawing-rooms. Their height may be regulated by the dimensions of the apartment in which they are placed, and from their vertical form they are well adapted to the Gothic style, which has been given in the annexed plate. The plan of the first is a triangle, supported by three griffins; and the two octagonals are decorated with pinnacles and flying buttresses.

Upright Plano-Forte, Music-Stand, and Chair
October 1826

UPRIGHT PLANO-FORTE, MUSIC-STAND, AND CHAIR

In the annexed plate are represented an upright piano-forte, a music-stand, and chair.

Having in a preceding portion of this work had occasion to treat of the horizontal piano we shall here only mention some peculiarities of an upright one.

From the little space which this instrument requires, it is admirably calculated for a small apartment, in which a horizontal piano would be heavy and inconvenient; it has also a very pleasing appearance when placed in a recess, such as that formed by the projection of the chimney; and, though so different in its form from the grand piano, it is nevertheless capable of producing the same pleasing sounds, but not in so powerful a tone.

The second subject in our plate is a music-desk. In consequence of the Roman Catholic service being chanted before the Reformation, a music-stand was to be found in all ecclesiastical edifices, from the chapel to the cathedral; but when, under Henry VIII. the mutilation and plunder of these edifices took place, few of the desks, which were mostly constructed in brass, escaped the rapacious and sacrilegious hand of avarice. But those few which still remain claim the admiration of every lover of ancient art. Among them there is none more entitled to our consideration than that of King's College, Cambridge, which, for beauty of workmanship, is not surpassed by the productions of the present day: but elegant as these specimens are, we have been obliged to differ from them in the present design, in order to render the stand more easy of removal; taking care, however, at the same time, to present the general character so beautiful in the originals.

The music-chair is constructed with a screw, so as to be capable of being raised or lowered like a stool; and it is decorated in the same style as the other pieces of furniture represented in the plate.

The material to be employed is rose-wood, inlaid with brass, and the space within the large circle, as well as that in the two square quatrefoils in the base, is of crimson silk.

55

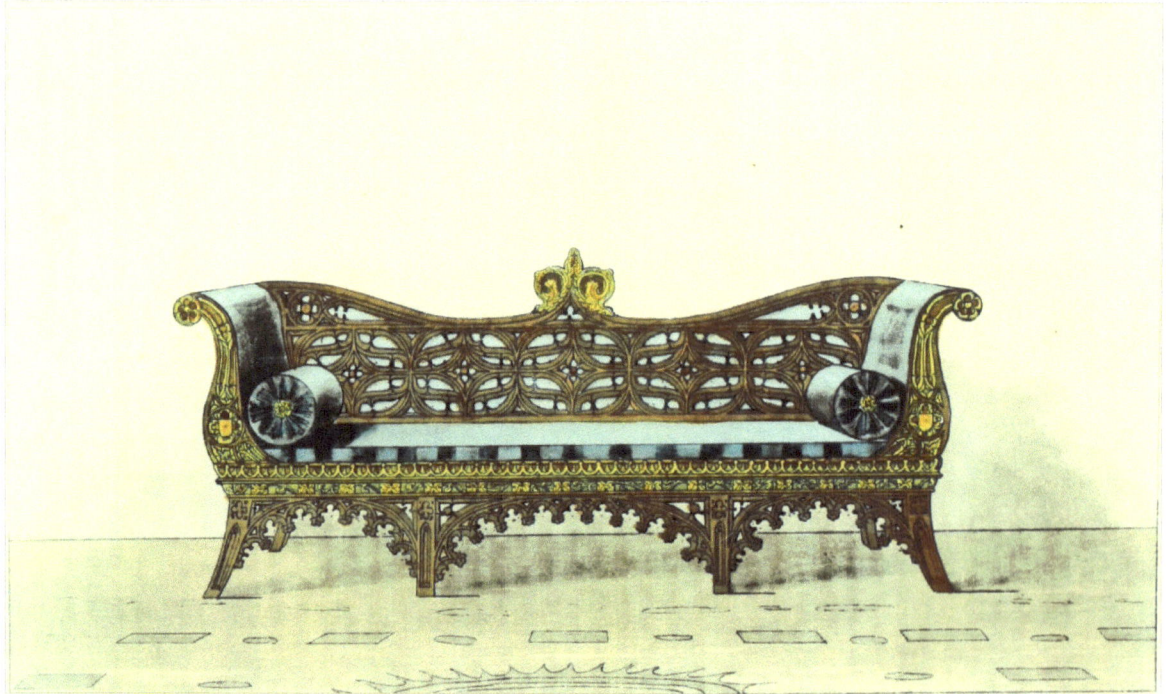

A Sofa
November 1826

A SOFA

The annexed plate represents a sofa decorated in the Gothic style. This piece of furniture is comparatively of modern date, and undoubtedly of Eastern origin; but in adapting it to European customs, it has been found necessary to vary the decoration in some degree from that of the original model.

In the Oriental countries a sofa is but little elevated from the floor, and consists of soft cushions covered with silk and other costly materials. Two of these are generally piled upon one another, and a third is placed against the wall to recline upon. These cushions are thus ranged round an apartment, and the heat of the climate renders them indispensable, either for public meetings or private assemblies. They are also well calculated for the sitting posture of the Eastern nations, which requires an easy couch. As none of these conveniences are adapted to the climate and customs of Europeans, the artist has been obliged to make some change from the original; so that the modern sofa presents quite a different appearance from its Oriental original: it nevertheless possesses a comfort which entitles it to rank among useful furniture. From its flowing and easy form, it is more calculated for the Italian than the Gothic style: the latter character has nevertheless been attempted to be given in the present design, which is composed from the best authorities in the florid style.

Gothic Chairs
December 1826

GOTHIC CHAIRS

There is no piece of furniture which is in more constant use than a chair: comfort ought therefore to be the principal consideration, at the same time blending so much elegance in its design as to render it a pleasing object in an apartment. The decoration of a chair ought undoubtedly to correspond with that of the situation in which it is placed: hence, those for a hall, dining-parlour, or drawing-room, should possess a totally different character: the first, that of simplicity; the second, a certain solidity, ornamented with appropriate decorations; and the third should combine elegance with lightness. The Gothic style will fully admit of these variations, and in the annexed plate a design for each has been given. There are but few specimens of the furniture of the sixteenth century remaining; those which once belonged to Cardinal Wolsey and a few others, now in the possession of his Majesty, are the only ones known to be extant; and even these are far from being pure in their details. They are executed in ebony, with ivory occasionally introduced in the heads of the figures, animals, &c. They are totally unfit for imitation, being clumsy in their design and very heavy. The use of chairs was hardly known to our ancestors, stools and benches being generally substituted in their place: so that in designing them for modern use, we must greatly deviate from their original character.

Gothic Looking-Glass
January 1827

GOTHIC LOOKING-GLASS

The design in this plate is intended to represent an upright moveable looking-glass, decorated in the florid style.

A looking-glass or mirror was a luxury unknown to our ancestors, as we learn from authentic sources that the Romans and other nations of antiquity used plates of brass, steel, and even silver, made perfectly smooth and highly polished. But although they produced a strong reflection, yet they are by no means comparable to this invention, by which, not only the labour of continual brightening is saved, but a much clearer reflection is produced. There is some uncertainty with respect to the actual period when mirrors were introduced; but it is well known that they were never brought to such perfection as at the present time. Venice was formerly the emporium of this manufacture, but France has for some time past furnished the greatest quantities, and latterly England equals (if not surpasses) any other nation in this kind of produce.

Great attention must be paid, in designing this piece of furniture, to give it a frame sufficiently solid to support the weight of so large a glass, without appearing heavy and ponderous. The artist has endeavoured to accomplish this object in the present design by the introduction of flying buttresses, which, while adding to the strength of the frame, detract nothing from the lightness of its character. The wood may be either rose or mahogany, and the ornaments of the same wood, or in or-moulu.

The moving glasses are now generally introduced in the sleeping-apartments and dressing-rooms of our nobility and persons of distinction.

58

A Gothic Bed
February 1827

A GOTHIC BED

    In a former part of this work, a design was given of a bed for a single person; but the present one is intended as a double or state-bed. It has long been a custom with the nobility of this country to be provided with a bed of this description, used only in case of being honoured with a visit from majesty or any other distinguished personage. As this custom is of very great antiquity, and as it existed at a time when Gothic architecture had attained the highest state of perfection, it may be presumed that no style can be more appropriate for decoration. It has been generally considered that the architecture of the middle ages possesses more playfulness in its outline, and richness in its details, than any other style: it is capable of being divided into two distinct classes, viz. ecclesiastical and domestic; and it is among the latter that we must refer for examples. From the ravages of time, few specimens of this kind earlier than the reign of Henry VII. are now remaining; therefore, in our decorations, we must conform as much as possible to the character of that period. To this effect, the artist has introduced the low four-centred arch so often found in edifices of that time, surmounted by a richly carved finial: the posts at the four angles are of an earlier date, and resemble the carving on the tomb of Crouchback in Westminster Abbey.

    The best materials for executing this design would be rose-wood and or-moulu, as mahogany is liable to become of too dark a tint. The colour of the draperies is left to the taste of the decorator, but they ought generally to correspond with that of the hangings.

Gothic Bookcase
March 1827

GOTHIC BOOKCASE

The library now constitutes one of the principal apartments in the country-seats of our noblemen and gentlemen. No style can be better adapted for its decoration than that of the middle ages, which possesses a sedate and grave character, that incites the mind to study and reflection. The rays passing through its variegated casements cast a religious light upon the venerable tomes on either side, the beautiful arrangements of its parts combining to produce an impressive grandeur in the whole design. Every thing proclaims it an apartment consecrated to learning. All mansions, however, are not sufficiently capacious to admit of devoting a whole apartment to this purpose: bookcases have therefore been resorted to, which form a most excellent substitute; as, while fulfilling the purpose of a library, they form handsome pieces of furniture, which can be well applied in filling up recesses and other inequalities in a room.

The Gothic style, it must be allowed, for the same reason as it is the most appropriate for a library, is also the best adapted for the decoration of these. The design given in the plate is of that taste; and its ornaments and details have been taken from the celebrated *Château Fontaine le Henri*, a mansion in Normandy, erected in the beginning of the sixteenth century. This edifice contains more scope for the decorator than we may say, perhaps, any other of the same period. From the peculiarity of its forms and the richness of its parts, this building may be considered as one of the best models of its kind.

Gothic Cabinet
April 1827

GOTHIC CABINET

The annexed plate represents a cabinet in the florid style. This piece of furniture has long since been introduced not only in the palaces of the great, but in humble habitations of the citizen and artisan. It is equally appropriate for the drawing-room and boudoir, and is capable of assuming different forms and characters, according to the style and destination of the room in which it is placed. Many of those made in the reign of Queen Elizabeth still remain to astonish the spectator by the intricacy of their parts, and to call forth his admiration by the beauty of their execution; but we believe few, if any, constructed prior to that period are still extant.

The most beautiful specimens of cabinets, however, are to be found among those denominated buhl and Florentine. The latter sort are particularly magnificent, the most costly woods, such as ebony, rose, mahogany, and cedar, being employed in their construction; whilst lapis lazuli and other precious stones are not unfrequently found in their decoration; and such is their costliness that on one alone many thousand pounds were expended in its execution. His present Majesty, we believe, has in his possession the most costly and extensive collection of any potentate in Europe, many of which are intended to enrich the furniture of the new palaces at Windsor and in London. The design is in the

Gothic character, and it is hoped will shew that that style is not unappropriate for its decoration: it is in rose-wood, and its ornaments and figures are in or-molu.

61

Description of a Bureau
May 1827

DESCRIPTION OF A BUREAU

The annexed plate is a bureau decorated in the Gothic style. It is appropriate either for a library or study, and is generally used for containing papers.

The centre part is divided into three equal compartments, terminating in pointed arches, and divided by buttresses, terminating in crocketed pinnacles, and above them the same divisions with very flat-headed arches; between these two tiers of panels are sliding drawers, the handles of which are formed out of the ornament in the quatrefoils.

The openings of these six compartments are filled up with silk, which should correspond with the colour of the apartment. At each extremity is a wing adorned with more complicated tracery, which is filled up with wood instead of the silk: these wings, which are terminated at each end with a buttress similar to the others, are surmounted by traceries in the form of flying buttresses. The ground-work may be of rose-wood or light oak, and the moulding and ornaments either gilt or in or-molu.

Library Table and Chair
June 1827

LIBRARY TABLE AND CHAIR

The form and decorations of tables are infinitely varied; and as they are equally introduced in the library, boudoir, dining, drawing, dressing rooms, &c. they partake of different characters suitable to the destination of the apartment in which they are placed. It is in France that the most elegant tables have been designed and executed, of which that of porcelain, presented to the Emperor Napoleon, is a magnificent specimen. The richest materials are sometimes employed in their construction; but mahogany and rose-wood are generally used, and sometimes ivory and other materials.

Respecting the tables of the middle ages little is known, but from the few documents which remain, they appear to have been very plain; and the rude state of the arts in those times amply justifies this opinion. Hence, in designing them in that style, the decorator is obliged to apply the Gothic decorations to modern forms.

The present design is intended for a library, to which is subjoined a chair in the same style. They may be executed either in light oak or rose-wood, and the ornaments in or-moulu.

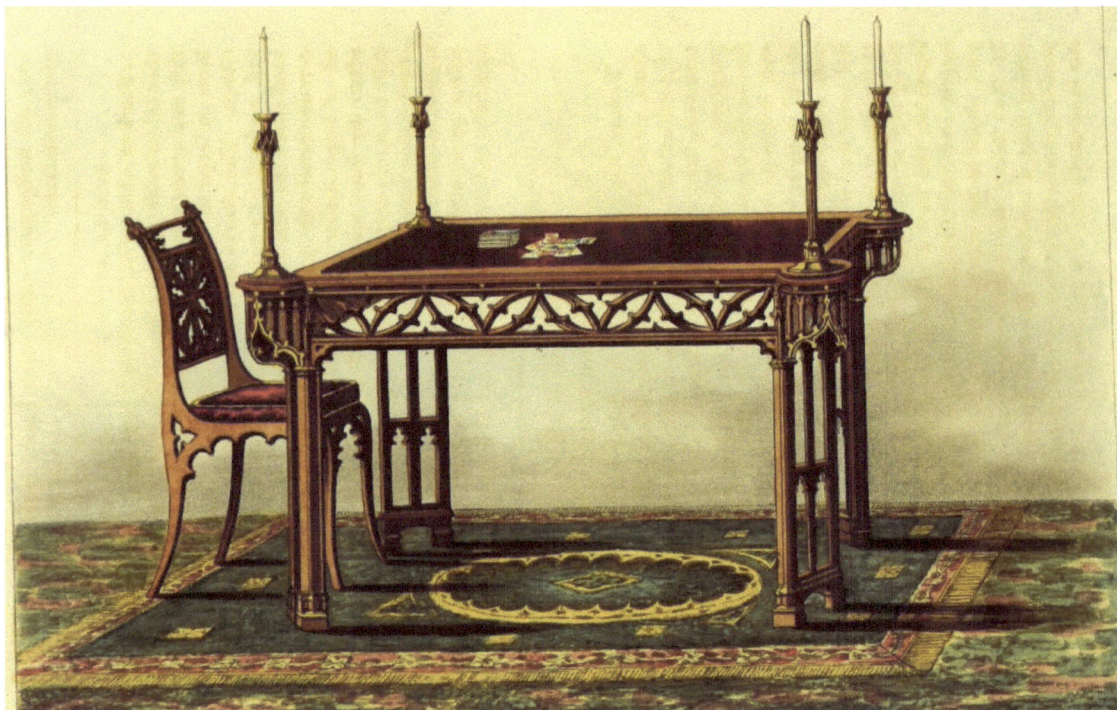

A Gothic Whist-Table
July 1827

A GOTHIC WHIST-TABLE

Tables, like other pieces of furniture, are capable of a great variety of combination in form, as well as in ornament, being intended for various purposes, and afford a great scope for the display of ingenuity and science in the mode of their support, as well as by enlarging or reducing them to any size. Till within these few years they were confined nearly to the same form, generally supported by four or more legs for the dining-room; but now a table of the largest size has often but one support, placed in the centre, avoiding by that means the inconvenience arising from a number. From the parallelogram to the circle every form has been used; and it is well known that what gave rise to the circular form was to avoid distinction among the guests.

The table selected for the plate is of a square form, for the purpose of playing at whist, having a projection at the angles, in order to place the candlesticks, which otherwise would have been in the way of the persons engaged at play. The style of its decorative parts is that of the fifteenth century. Great Britain exhibits more magnificence in this kind of furniture than any other country in Europe, particularly in the style, being the only country at present where this beautiful style of architecture is understood.

A Gothic Toilette
August 1827

A GOTHIC TOILETTE

There are now extant very few articles of furniture, if any, beyond the time of Queen Elizabeth, the style of which, it is well known, differs widely from that of the early part of Henry VIII. as at that period a total change took place in architecture, and, of course, in all the minor branches. The Roman and Gothic were united, and formed a sort of mixed style, possessing neither the grandeur of the former, nor the taste of the latter: therefore, for want of examples, the decorator must select from architectural remains and from combinations which unite fitness with truth of character.

In the annexed design, which represents a lady's toilette, or dressing-table, the artist has endeavoured to preserve the true domestic Gothic form and details, and to avoid the ecclesiastical style, which has too often been adopted in some of the mansions of our noblemen and gentlemen. As the pointed arch is a leading feature of the ecclesiastical architecture, the flat or elliptical should be adopted in preference; for which reason the top of the glass is made of a four-centred arch, surmounted with crockets and a finial, having a perforated projection on each side, adorned with traceries, which serve both as a support and ornament. The drawers placed under the glass, as well as the table, partake of the same character: the latter is supported at the four corners by slender pillars, surmounted in front by three very flat arches, above which a great variety of tracery is introduced. Rose or fancy wood may be used; a few of the principal ornaments to be in or-molu. The tracery requires very little projection.

We have now so many skilful workmen in Gothic, that very elaborate pieces of furniture may be made at a moderate price, compared with what it was a few years ago.

65

Gothic Utensils
September 1827

GOTHIC UTENSILS

The annexed plate represents various utensils, such as keys, hearth-broom, bell-pull, &c. &c. The two keys were made in the early part of the sixteenth century, and are in the writer's possession; the other articles are in imitation of the florid Gothic style, which is better calculated for small objects, from the variety and intricacy of its ornaments. Owing to the discovery of the ruins of Pompeii and Herculaneum, we possess some specimens of the furniture and utensils of the Greeks and Romans; but there are very few left of the middle ages. Many of the age of Elizabeth are now in perfect preservation, but scarcely any previous to her time. The Gothic style begins to be well understood in this country; and we have very superior workmen in its various branches, which we owe, in a great measure, to the encouragement given by his late, as well as his present, Majesty, as may be seen in the great and magnificent works in progress at Windsor Castle.

Gothic Furniture
October 1827

GOTHIC FURNITURE

The accompanying print exhibits collectively those articles of furniture which have already been represented in detail in the late Numbers of the *Repository*. It displays the appearance of an apartment fitted up in the general style of the fifteenth century, but with those improved forms and elegant contrivances which the superiority of modern art and ingenuity have introduced. The combination and fitness of the whole are highly pleasing; and the decorations, being less massive than those in use among our ancestors, produce a lightness of effect better suited to the apartments of our gay and lively fashionables, than the solemn gloom which accompanied the grandeur of the middle ages.

The Gothic style, which we have shewn to be so well adapted to domestic arrangements and decorations, is becoming much more general than it was a few years since. We have the satisfaction of believing, that the designs, which have appeared from time to time in this work, have contributed to extend this growing taste; and, for its further encouragement, those designs, with the letter-press descriptions, are preparing for publication in a separate volume, which is expected to prove of considerable interest and assistance, as well to upholsterers and other professional persons, as to the admirers of the Gothic style by whom they are employed.

Drawing-Room Chairs
February 1828

DRAWING-ROOM CHAIRS

Judging from the admirable ancient remains of the Egyptians, the Greeks, and the Romans, we may infer that those nations were equally magnificent in their decorations and furniture; but as we have no examples transmitted to us, it is only by tradition we know that among them chairs were occasionally used by the higher class of people. These were made of rich materials, such as ebony, ivory, &:c.; but it is a matter of doubt if they were more than stools, or used as thrones, having no back to them. It is well known, that to this day the inhabitants of the East hardly use chairs, but recline on cushions, sofas, and ottomans; and though they are used in China, they are by no means so common there as in European countries. In the 15th and 16th centuries, chairs were not so much in use as they are now; they were made large, clumsy, and stiff in appearance, no curved lines being then introduced in the making of them. The modern chairs, though much smaller, are made stronger than those before-mentioned, which is owing to the introduction of curved lines. In Catholic countries, chairs are made use of in churches instead of pews; and even in the public walks persons are accommodated with chairs, but of a very common sort.

In the accompanying plate are represented two chairs, fit to be placed in a drawing-room, requiring richness and elegance in their designs. They both bear the same character, differing only in size, and in the addition of elbows. The blue silk is to correspond with the hanging of the room. Part of the ornaments are carved in wood, and the smallest in metal, of or-molu: the body of the chair should be made of fancy wood.

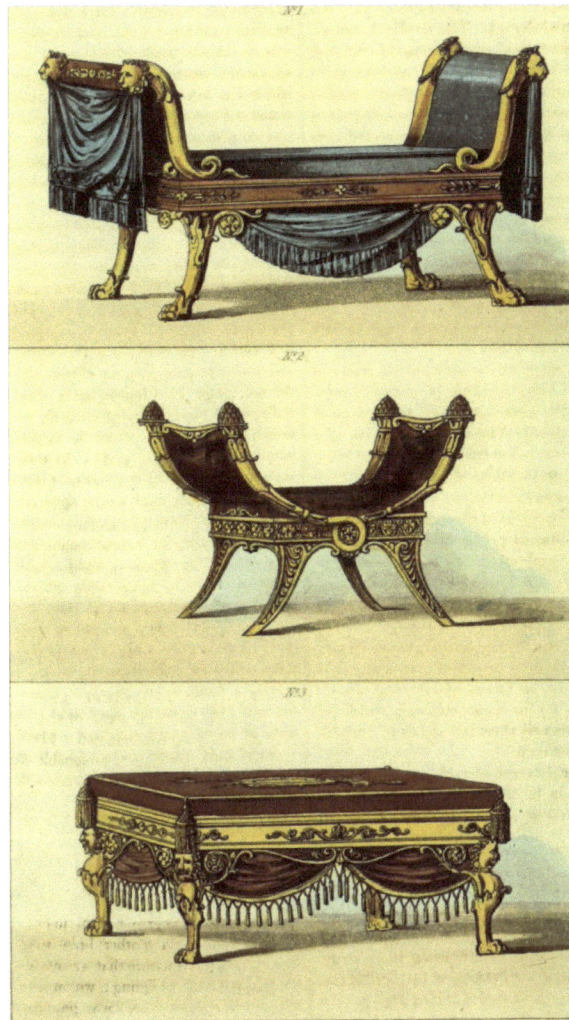

Drawing-Room Seats
March 1828

DRAWING-ROOM SEATS

The annexed plate represents three seats intended for a drawing-room, on account of the richness of their ornaments and the lightness of their framing.

No. 1. retains a French name, and is generally called *causette*, probably owing to its admitting two persons to sit upon it. In decoration, as in other branches of art, it is only in nature that we must seek materials in designing: we must therefore refer to the animal or vegetable kingdom tor subjects of embellishment. The tops of the two sides are adorned with tour lions' heads, and the four legs with claws: the other ornaments are leaves and flowers in or-moulu, variously combined. The stuff and draperies are the same as the hangings of the room: fancy-wood forms the framing of it.

No. 2. is calculated for one person alone. Seats of this kind were formerly more in use than chairs; and even as late as the reign of Louis XVI. it was customary to say, speaking of a courtier,

" *C'est un home comme il faut,, il a tabouret chez le roi."* It is only within the last thirty or forty years that plain or arm-chairs have been so generally used; they were a luxury almost unknown to our ancestors.

No. 3. is a window-seat, which is generally placed in the recesses of windows, and made to fit the apertures; it is in every respect like the two former, with the exception that it has no sides to it. The lion is introduced as a symbol of strength, which is considered as a proper characteristic for a seat which has a constant bearing.

69

Toilette
April 1828

TOILETTE

We are now making use of a number of articles of furniture which were unknown to our ancestors; but the toilette, which is the subject of the annexed plate, takes its origin from the most remote antiquity. It is placed in the *sanctum sanctorum* of the English lady, called the dressing-room, where it serves principally to reflect the charms of the fair, who is to command, by its assistance, the admiration of every beholder. On the Continent, and particularly in France, the dressing-room is open to every visiter, from the poet and artist, to the politician and prelate; and where all subjects are submitted and discussed previous to their being given to the world. In those countries, the toilette is considered as the altar of fashion, where every one deposits his tribute at the feet of the enchantress, who gives laws in the sanctuary of elegance and taste.

As the wish to please is inherent in our nature, we cannot therefore be surprised if, so many of the fair sex spend hours in adding to the charms which they already possess, and in assisting nature by the bewitching hand of fashion.

The toilette ought to be light in its general character and diversity of materials, elegant in design; and it has been the endeavour of the artist to unite these qualifications in the present design.

70

A Side Board
May 1828

A SIDE-BOARD

Nature in all its laws requires action and reaction: therefore men, in common with all other animals, cannot live without a constant supply of food. It is not only necessary, but also our greatest pleasure arises from gratifying those inclinations. It is not to be wondered at that we spend a great portion of our time, not only in supporting nature, but likewise in indulging our appetite, and insensibly carrying the luxury of the table to the highest degree of refinement and elegance.

Individuals, as well as nations, are endeavouring to surpass each other in the sumptuousness of their feasts, and every thing connected with them. The buffet or side-board, which takes its leading share, by its presenting to the eye the combined display of the produce of nature and of art, and in all the variety and richness of their forms, concurs in producing a most pleasing effect.

The present design forms a parallelogram, divided into three parts, the centre of which is a semicircular arch, resting on a socle, which forms the base of the four pilasters placed on both sides. The ornaments are of a Grecian character, composed chiefly of the honeysuckle, lions' heads, &c.; and carved of the same wood.

In the middle of the semicircular arch is placed a circular wine-cooler, resting on four chimeras; a light grey marble slab is placed on the top.

A Sofa
June 1828

A SOFA

Nature having collected all her treasures in the Eastern part of the world, it is from the East we obtain both the ideas and the articles for our furniture, as well as for the dazzling and precious ornaments of our persons. In every clime riches and luxury produce habits of indolence and indulgence; and these, being fostered by the excessive heat of the Eastern climate, have obtained for us that elegant and luxurious piece of furniture called a sofa, which was doubtless invented by the natives of the East, on account of its allowing a reclined position, which of all others affords the most relief to the body, when overcome by lassitude or fatigue. For this reason, as well as for its elegant form, the sofa has been adopted among all civilized nations; so that from the palace to the cottage *ornée*, it is now required in
every room, and may therefore rank among the leading articles of our modern furniture.

The annexed plate represents a sofa, suited by the richness of its parts for a drawing-room; and it will be perceived that undulating lines have been preferred in its design to straight ones, both as being more pleasing to the eye, and as contributing more to the ease of the person sitting or reclining thereon.

The design here given is calculated for four persons to sit with ease. The colour of the drapery must depend on the fittings up of the room; but in all cases the lions' paws, which form the support, as also the ornaments carved in wood, must be gilt.

Fire-Place
July 1828

FIRE-PLACE

It is well known that fire-places were not in use among the Egyptians or the Greeks, and were very little used by the Romans, the heat of their climate not requiring fires; but in Europe, and towards the poles, it is one of the most requisite appendages to the interior arrangements of a room. Fire-places have varied with the fashion of the times; for towards the beginning of the 17th century they were made of very large dimensions, compared with our present size; and they were enriched to some height with sculptures, representing allegorical subjects, or ornaments. Towards the latter part of the 17th century looking-glasses came much into use; they were ultimately placed above the fire-place, for which reason a new character of decoration was adopted, as they were made low enough to allow persons to see themselves reflected therein.

In this country we introduce fire-places in almost every room; great attention has therefore been paid to their improvement, both in regard to the mode of their construction as well as decoration. The jambs and mantel-piece are generally made of various kinds of marble, ornamented more or less according to the decoration of the room for which they are intended.

One of the greatest comforts to be obtained, and at the same time one of the greatest difficulties to be overcome, consists in the erection of fire places in such a manner as to be free from smoke. A great variety of plans have for many years been tried, though without success; and it is only very lately that this great nuisance has been overpowered by the very ingenious discovery of Mr. Hiort, of his Majesty's Office of Works, who, by a long and able experience, has at last invented a method for getting rid of this very great inconvenience, which not only affects the health of individuals, but likewise injures every article of furniture.

This discovery forms an epoch in architecture, as by its adoption the architect is not compelled to raise his shafts higher than he wishes; and it obviates the necessity of spoiling the appearance of the roof by a number of shafts, rising one above another, as in the water-front of Somerset-House.

FIRE-PLACE - Continued

The fire-place represented in the plate is calculated for a drawing-room of a moderate size, and rather plain in its decorations. The jambs and mantel-piece are of black marble, with figures and ornaments relieved in or-moulu. The slab is also of the same materials, projecting about six inches, in order to leave room, for placing vases, clocks, &c. Above it is a looking-glass corresponding in width to the opening of the chimney. The stove is made of polished steel, relieved by Grecian ornaments in or-moulu; and the fender is entirely of that metal, in order to harmonize with the richness, of the figures placed on the jambs.

Drawing-Room-Table
August 1828

DRAWING-ROOM-TABLE

The annexed plate represents a drawing-room-table, decorated in the Grecian style. The form of its base is triangular, from which rises a perpendicular pillar, supporting the framing of the table. The stand and mouldings of the rim are intended to be carved in mahogany; but the top may be veneered with some fancy wood, with an inlaid border.

There are several distinct sorts of tables, each of which has its own particular character. The dining-table (which may be either circular or parallelogram) should have great strength, and ought to be so constructed as to lengthen or decrease at pleasure, so that the size of the table may be suited to the number of persons placed at it. This, as well as most tables, is now supported by a pillar in the centre, which is a great modern improvement, as it prevents the confinement of the legs arising from the old-fashioned method of support.

There are likewise sofa, occasional library, and pier tables, each of which must partake of the character of the apartment in which it is placed: but as these have already been severally described, it would be superfluous to dilate further upon them.

PIER-TABLE
September 1828

PIER-TABLE

The position and use of a pier- table are obvious from its appellation; namely, to stand against the piers or portions of wall between windows.

The forms and decorations of pier-tables may be infinitely varied. Some are covered with slabs of porphyry or verd-antique marble; some with curiously inlaid woods; others, denominated buhl, are entirely decorated with tortoiseshell and brass: but their forms are equally varied with their ornament.

Some are canted at the ends of the front, as in the present design; others are parallelograms, supported by griffins, chimeras, terms, or lyres, as in the annexed plate; others again rest on brackets, springing from the wall, in order not to encroach on the space of the floor. These differences, however, are mostly to be regulated by localities, and must therefore be determined by the science and judgment of the architect.

The present design, which embraces nearly the whole space between the windows, may be executed either in mahogany or rose- wood, enriched with gilding or or-molu. At the back is a looking-glass, in order both to lighten the design and to give an appearance of distance, where it would otherwise appear heavy.

The vases and clock are only accessories, and not intended to form any part of the principal design.

A Bed
October 1828

A BED

The design of a bed in the annexed plate is in the Grecian style, and is constructed on those light and elegant principles introduced by the French, on the revival of Grecian architecture. The decorations are entirely in that taste, which it is to be hoped, for the honour of modern art, will eventually supersede the heavy, cumbrous, and, we may almost add, unmeaning, decorations of the style denominated that of Louis XIV. The present design is intended to be executed in mahogany; but it may be enriched with gilding without any impropriety.

The draperies are to be attached to the decorated cornice, behind which is concealed the rod on which the bed-curtains run. The reason why the French so far exceed us in the beauty and decorations of their beds, may be attributed to a custom peculiar to that nation of receiving visiters in their sleeping apartments: but it is to be hoped that the ancient custom of having state-beds, which once formed an important feature in the palaces and mansions of our nobility, will be revived.

A Flower-Stand
November 1828

A FLOWER-STAND

Among those pieces of furniture which unite the beauties of nature and art none is more conspicuous than the flower-stand. It is equally appropriate for the drawing-room, library, and boudoir, and is likewise employed on a larger scale in the conservatory. In France and Italy, where the heat of the climate requires all that is cool and refreshing, flower-stands are much used; and occasionally small artificial fountains are introduced in them, which by their continual action cool the air, and refresh the plants placed around them. Thus the flower-stand is rendered at once a useful, pleasing, and ornamental piece of furniture, and may be considered as almost indispensable in the refined mansions of modern times.

The annexed design is of an equilateral triangular form, and is intended to be executed in white or veined marble, from the supposition that its coldness will be more congenial to the plants which are placed in it.

A Cabinet
December 1828

A CABINET

Cabinets, in common with all the works of human ingenuity, have, since their invention, been formed into a variety of shapes and adapted to as great a variety of purposes, they being in the present day made use of equally for the subordinate as for the more magnificent apartments of the palace or mansion. In former times, about the 14th and 15th centuries, they were used solely for the purpose of depositing relics, or missals, or some one or other of those trifles upon which fanatics placed so high a value, and which they regarded with so great reverence; consequently they were wrought with the greatest possible costliness, being really surprising for their beauty of composition and the excellence of their workmanship. At present they serve for repositories of the most costly articles of apparel, such as jewels, trinkets, &c.; and shells, minerals, insects, and other specimens of natural history; and also of exquisitely illuminated missals and other curious relics of antiquity, probably the same they formerly contained, though for a very different and more interesting purpose.

The annexed design is about three feet high, and has fanciful columns at each end, supporting an entablature enriched with ornaments. In the centre is a slender pillar, enriched with a cornucopia. On each side of the two panels: is a sort of laurel, at each angle; and the work in the centre represents sunrise. On the top, at some distance back, are small drawers, or spaces open to receive books, &c.

The bases of the columns rest upon a socle of varied form, which returns on each side as far as the wall, about three feet.

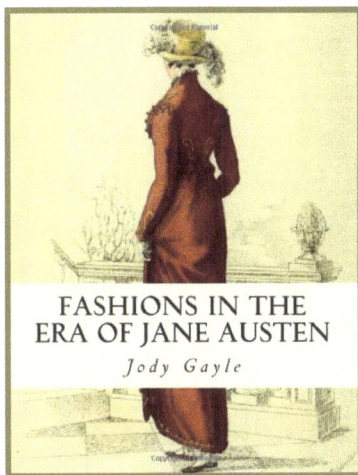

My love of historical romance novels inspired me to do research about nineteenth century England. Finding Ackermann's *Repository of Arts* sparked my curiosity and every since I have been dedicated to unearthing, publishing and reintroducing one of the most influential periodicals of Jane Austen's lifetime – Ackermann's *Repository of Arts*.

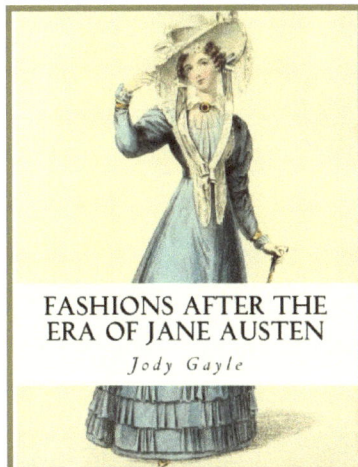

These books in the series *Era of Jane Austen* are a pictorial of images accompanied by the original descriptions, as published more than two hundred years ago. The illustrations and the period's language assists historical romance readers to add depth to the visualizations we each create while reading a novel.

Costume designers, researchers, authors, and enthusiasts will all treasure these authentic examples of fashionable dress, furniture and draperies in the era of Jane Austen.

I hope everyone enjoys these pictorials as much as I have loved putting them together!

Jody Gayle

Fashions in the Era of Jane Austen
What gown would you have worn to be the belle of the ball in April 1811?

Fashions in the Era of Jane Austen covers twelve years of fashion in the Georgian and Regency periods...morning, evening, riding, and walking dresses with their coordinated accessories: hats, shoes, scarves, jewelry, parasols and more.

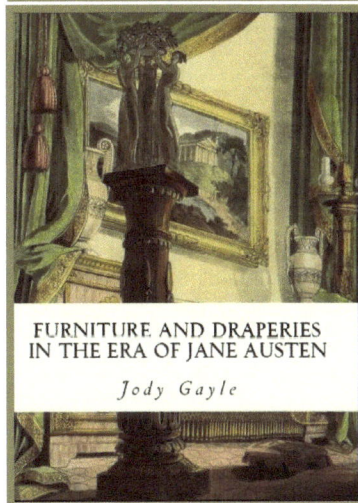

Fashions After the Era of Jane Austen
What carriage gown would you have worn for a ride in a phaeton through Hyde Park in April, 1826?"?

Fashions After the Era of Jane Austen covers seven years of fashions in the late Georgian period (1821-1828) ...morning, evening, riding, and walking dresses with their coordinated accessories: hats, shoes, scarves, jewelry, parasols and more.

Furniture and Draperies in the Era of Jane Austen
In chapter after chapter, Austen utilized furniture to craft scenes and create drama by directing her characters around the room, to and from chairs, sofas, windows, fireplaces and even the pianoforte.

Furniture and Draperies in the Era of Jane Austen covers twelve years of fashionable furniture and draperies in the Georgian and Regency period (1809-1820).

Needlework Patterns in the Era of Jane Austen
What would Jane Austen have stitched, while seated in her drawing room and waiting for callers?

Needlework Patterns in the Era of Jane Austen covers twelve years of fashion embroidery designs in the Georgian and Regency period (1809-1820).

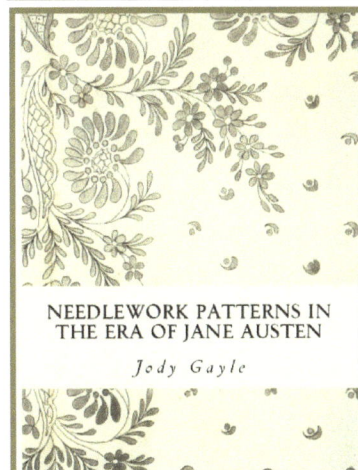

JODY GAYLE, bestselling author and researcher, likens her work to that of a literary archeologist rather than a traditional author or imperator of history. She is dedicated to unearthing publications of the past, and sharing these long-forgotten books... the jewels and riches of the written word. She has uncovered tens of thousands of old publications from the eighteenth and nineteenth centuries and wants to bring them to life, and send her readers traveling back in time.

About Jody...

* She grew up on a farm in a small town of about 500 people and first learned to drive on a tractor. She can milk a cow as easily as pluck a chicken.

* Stood within twenty feet of the first node of the International Space Station. Unfortunately, her feet were firmly planted on the earth at the time.

* Has gone whitewater rafting and horseback riding in the mountains of Montana. She has swum with dolphins and sharks, and refueled a fighter jet in the sky on an Air Force KC135. Jody is a bit of an adventurer.

* Jody and her son share the same birthday -- New Year's Day!

She loves to hear from her readers. Visit her website and Facebook page.

Thank you for reading
FASHIONS IN THE ERA OF JANE AUSTEN

If you enjoyed this book, I would appreciate it if you'd help other readers enjoy it, too. After all, most books are purchased due to word-of-mouth recommendations. How can you help?

Recommend it. Please help other readers find this book by recommending it to friends, readers' groups, and discussion boards.

Review it. Please tell other readers why you liked this book by reviewing it on Amazon, Goodreads, or your blog. If you write a review, please send me a copy at jody@jodygayle.com